DAVID R. ROSS has so far managed to refrain from inscribing 'There goes biker Dave' on the back of his leather jacket for those times when he zooms on his erratic travels from historic site to crash to breakdown to historic site. Small children ask him 'Why do you ride an 1100cc bike which can go at silly speeds, biker Dave?' Sagely he replies, 'Who wants to ride a carthorse when you can ride a thoroughbred?'

David R. Ross (the R, by the way, is for Robertson, his mother's maiden name) was extremely well educated. He went to a good school – it was approved. He describes himself as 'not very bright, but I do enjoy lifting heavy things'. At school his head was full of dominoes which were mostly chapping, but he has always had a penchant for unearthing details about Scotland and its history which he absorbs and then spills out with monotonous regularity, much to the despair of everyone who knows him. Indeed, his whole life seems to consist of boring people with historical data interspersed with dreadful old jokes. He genuinely believes he was born at the wrong time, or at least that's the excuse he uses every time he is apprehended by the polis whilst walking the streets armed with a collection of medieval weaponry. He is currently convenor of the Society of William Wallace and is renowned for his startling and ground-breaking approach to public speaking. He often regales audiences with tales of his adventures on historic properties, especially the one about being escorted off the premises with head held high – and feet held even higher.

David's favourite drink, other than Belgian beer, is whisky and lemonade (no ice). It's a dreadful way to drink whisky, he says, but a great way to drink lemonade. David resides in East Kilbride – serves him right.

By the same author:
On the Trail of William Wallace (1999)
On the Trail of Robert the Bruce (1999)
A Passion for Scotland (2002)

D0988040

On the Trail of
Bonnie Prince Charlie

DAVID R. ROSS

Luath Press Limited

EDINBURGH

www.luath.co.uk

First Edition 2000
Reprinted 2002

The paper used in this book is acid-free, neutral-sized and recyclable.
It is made from low chlorine pulps produced in a low-energy, low
emission manner from renewable forests.

Printed and bound by
Bell & Bain Ltd., Glasgow

Typeset in 10.5 point Sabon by
S. Fairgrieve, Edinburgh, 0131 658 1763

Line drawings by Anthony Fury

Maps and battle plans by Jim Lewis

I was in the coffeehouse with Smollett when the news of the battle of Culloden arrived, and when London all over was in a perfect uproar of joy... I asked Smollett if he was ready to go, as he lived at Mayfair; he said he was, and would conduct me. The mob were so riotous, and the squibs so numerous and incessant that we were glad to go into a narrow entry to put our wigs in our pockets and to take our swords from our belts and walk with them in our hands, as everybody then wore swords; and, after cautioning me against speaking a word, lest the mob should discover my country and become insolent, 'for John Bull,' says he, 'is as haughty and valiant tonight as he was abject and cowardly on the Black Wednesday when the Highlanders were at Derby.' After we got to the head of the Haymarket through incessant fire, the Doctor led me by narrow lanes, where we met nobody but a few boys at a pitiful bonfire, who very civilly asked us for sixpence, which I gave them. I saw not Smollett for some time after, when he showed Smith and me the manuscript of his Tears of Scotland, which was published not long after, and had such a run of approbation.

Alexander Carlyle
London, 1746

The Tears of Scotland

Tobias Smollett

Mourn, hapless Caledonia, mourn
Thy banish'd peace, thy laurels torn!
Thy sons, for valour long renown'd,
Lie slaughter'd on their native ground;
Thy hospitable roofs no more
Invite the stranger to the door;
In smoky ruins sunk they lie,
The monuments of cruelty.

The wretched owner sees afar
His all become they prey of war;
Bethinks him of his babes and wife,
Then smites his breast and curses life.
Thy swains are famish'd on the rocks,
Where once they fed their wanton flocks;
Thy ravish'd virgins shriek in vain;
Thy infants perish on the plain.

What boots it then, in every clime,
Through the wide spreading waste of time,
Thy martial glory, crown'd with praise,
Still shone with undiminish'd blaze?
Thy tow'ring spirit now is broke,
Thy neck is bended to the yoke.
What foreign arms could never quell,
By civil rage and rancour fell.

The rural pipe and merry lay
No more shall cheer the happy day;
No social scenes of gay delight

Beguile the dreary winter night;
No strains but those of sorrow flow,
And nought be heard but sounds of woe,
While the pale phantoms of the slain
Glide nightly o'er the silent plain.

O baneful cause, oh! fatal morn,
Accurs'd to ages yet unborn!
The sons against their father stood,
The parent shed his children's blood.
Yet, when the rage of battle ceas'd
The victor's soul was not appeas'd;
The naked and forlorn must feel
Devouring flames, and murd'ring steel!

The pious mother, doom'd to death,
Forsaken, wanders o'er the heath;
The bleak wind whistles round her head,
Her helpless orphans cry for bread;
Bereft of shelter, food, and friend,
She views the shades of night descend;
And stretch'd beneath th' inclement skies,
Weeps o'er her tender babes, and dies.

While the warm blood bedews my veins,
And unimpair'd remembrance reigns,
Resentment of my country's fate
Within my filial breast shall beat;

And, spite of her insulting foe,
My sympathizing verse shall flow:
"Mourn, hapless Caledonia, mourn
Thy banish'd peace, thy laurels torn."

Acknowledgements

I AM HUGELY INDEBTED to W. Drummond Norie who released a four-volume account, *The Life and Adventures of Prince Charles Edward Stuart,* after a tour he made in 1899. His works gave me an early grounding in the actual route taken by Charles's forces and enabled me to visit the various sites. For anyone who wants an intimate account of Charles's wanderings as a fugitive after Culloden, it is a valuable guidebook. Mention should also be made of the more recent *The Prince in the Heather* by Eric Linklater, another post-Culloden account. In addition to the books referred to above and in the bibliography, I used maps of every age and description, and a wealth of information was gained on the hoof, so to speak, asking questions of people in various localities and inquiring at local information offices and museums at the various towns visited.

Thanks as always to Karen and Kimberley, Dick Clark and Linda Donnelly; Catriona Scott, editor; Bob McCutcheon, Bookseller of Stirling, for his stories and guidance, and for generously allowing me to reproduce photographs and illustrations from books in his extensive collection, in particular:

Vues Pittoresques de l'Écosse A Pichot (text), F.A. Pernot (engravings), 1827
Pictorial History of Scotland James Taylor, 1859
Border Antiquities of England and Scotland Walter Scott, 1814
Scotland Illustrated Dr William Beattie (text), T. Alcom, W.H. Bartlett and H. McCulloch (illustrations), 1838;

Aero Leathers of Galashiels for their rufty-tufty motorcycle clothing that has seen me bounce along tarmac without a scratch to skin or clothes; Armour Class of Yoker, Glasgow, who crafted the many weapons that I use during talks (including the Wallace sword on the cover of *On the Trail of William Wallace*); Joe Lindsay, Targemaker of North Kessock; Davie White and the boys at the John Wright Sports Centre gym who taught me what bench press is really all about, and 'slagged' me to death at the same time; The Society of William Wallace; and all at Luath Press for withstanding my blunt-headed blunt-headedness.

Contents

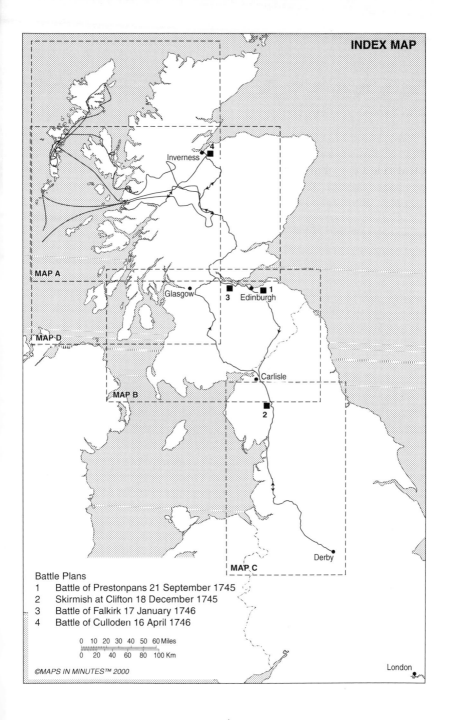

INDEX MAP

Inverness

4

Glasgow

3 Edinburgh

1

MAP A

MAP D

Carlisle

MAP B

2

Derby

MAP C

Battle Plans
1   Battle of Prestonpans 21 September 1745
2   Skirmish at Clifton 18 December 1745
3   Battle of Falkirk 17 January 1746
4   Battle of Culloden 16 April 1746

0   10 20 30 40 50 60 Miles
0   20   40   60   80   100 Km

©MAPS IN MINUTES™ 2000

London

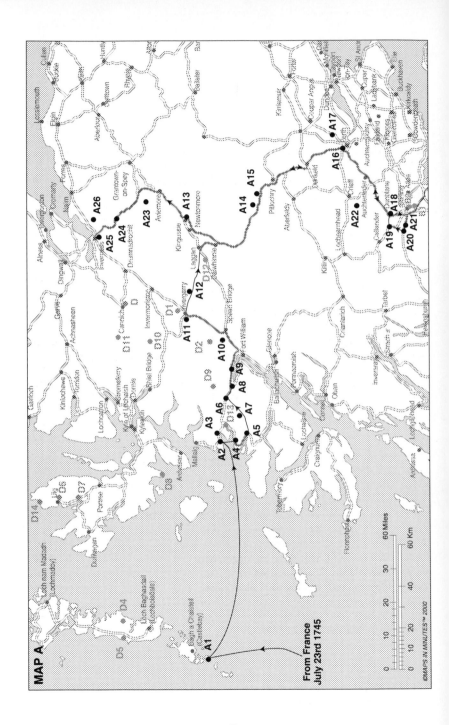

MAP A

From France
July 23rd 1745

©MAPS IN MINUTES™ 2000

Key to Map A

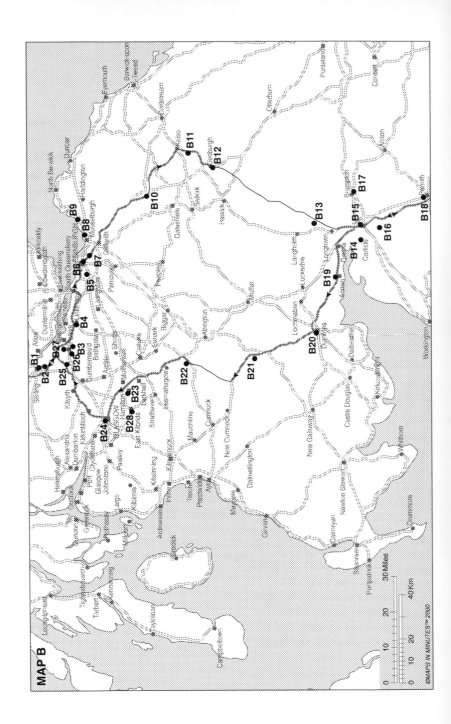

MAP B

Key to Map B

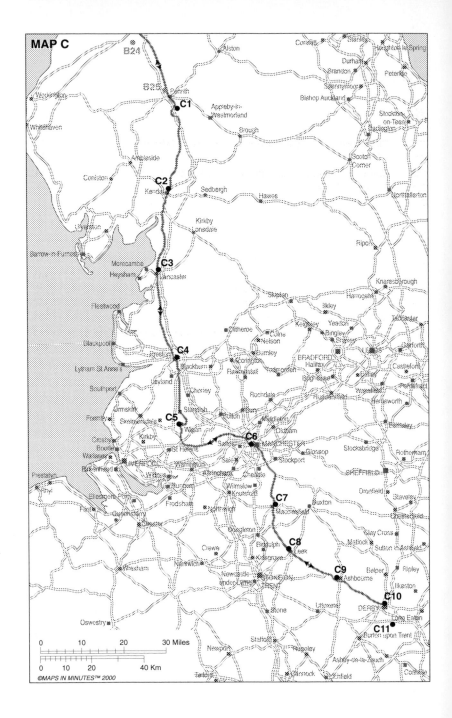

MAP C

xvi

Key to Map C

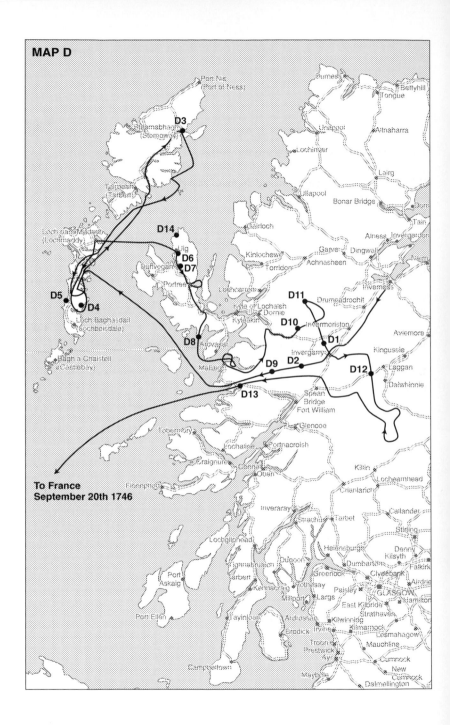

MAP D

To France
September 20th 1746

xviii

Key to Map D

Foreword

AFTER WRITING *On the Trail of William Wallace* and *On the Trail of Robert the Bruce*, this was a very different book to work on. William Wallace and Robert the Bruce are heroes in Scotland. Charles Edward Stuart is seen in a different light completely. When I mentioned to people that I was working on a book about him, some were quite vitriolic in their views. His personality, his aims, and the lasting effect he had on Scotland were the subjects mainly raised. But there is an air of romanticism connected with him, and the time he spent walking the landscape of Scotland has gone down in folklore. Behind all the character assassination, it is still acknowledged that he was the rightful heir to the throne.

Religion is a rather touchy subject in Scotland. I have shied away from religious and political machinations in this story as much as possible – there are many other works that can fill in these details. I wanted to make this a simple, accessible book, telling Charles's story through places more than anything else.

Life would be very dull indeed for me if I walked and drove round the country not knowing the events that had taken place wherever I found myself. If this book can bring the landscape to life for you, and perhaps even inspire you to visit some of the places mentioned, then I have done the job I set out to do.

One detail should perhaps be borne in mind when ascending Highland hillsides during the summer months. I have had some horrific experiences during my life with that Scots equivalent to the Tasmanian Devil – the Highland Midge. There is a famous story that when Charles started to wear the plaid as his everyday apparel, he commented that all he needed was an itch to make him a complete Highlander. Writers have always assumed that this was a reference to the common belief that Highlanders were flea-ridden. I think it's more likely they were scratching their midgie bites!

David R. Ross
August 2000

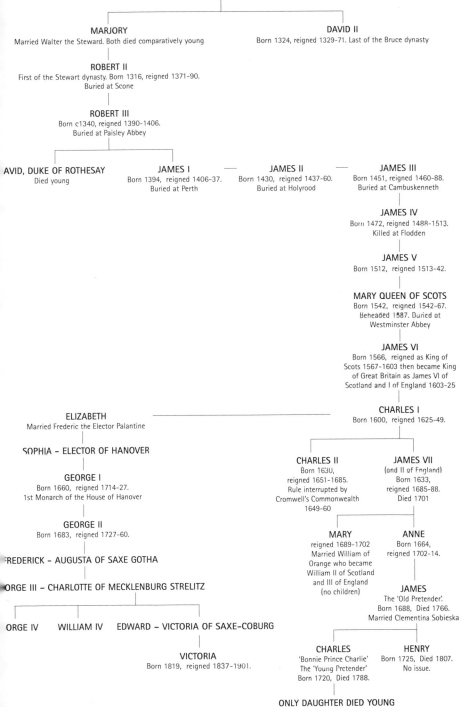

ROBERT THE BRUCE, HERO KING OF SCOTS
Born 1274, reigned 1306–29. Buried in Dunfermline Abbey

MARJORY
Married Walter the Steward. Both died comparatively young

DAVID II
Born 1324, reigned 1329-71. Last of the Bruce dynasty

ROBERT II
First of the Stewart dynasty. Born 1316, reigned 1371-90.
Buried at Scone

ROBERT III
Born c1340, reigned 1390-1406.
Buried at Paisley Abbey

AVID, DUKE OF ROTHESAY
Died young

JAMES I
Born 1394, reigned 1406-37.
Buried at Perth

JAMES II
Born 1430, reigned 1437-60.
Buried at Holyrood

JAMES III
Born 1451, reigned 1460-88.
Buried at Cambuskenneth

JAMES IV
Born 1472, reigned 1488-1513.
Killed at Flodden

JAMES V
Born 1512, reigned 1513-42.

MARY QUEEN OF SCOTS
Born 1542, reigned 1542-67.
Beheaded 1587. Buried at
Westminster Abbey

JAMES VI
Born 1566, reigned as King of
Scots 1567-1603 then became King
of Great Britain as James VI of
Scotland and I of England 1603-25

ELIZABETH
Married Frederic the Elector Palatine

CHARLES I
Born 1600, reigned 1625-49.

SOPHIA – ELECTOR OF HANOVER

GEORGE I
Born 1660, reigned 1714-27.
1st Monarch of the House of Hanover

CHARLES II
Born 1630,
reigned 1651-1685.
Rule interrupted by
Cromwell's Commonwealth
1649-60

JAMES VII
(and II of England)
Born 1633,
reigned 1685-88.
Died 1701

GEORGE II
Born 1683, reigned 1727-60.

MARY
reigned 1689-1702
Married William of
Orange who became
William II of Scotland
and III of England
(no children)

ANNE
Born 1664,
reigned 1702-14.

FREDERICK – AUGUSTA OF SAXE GOTHA

ORGE III – CHARLOTTE OF MECKLENBURG STRELITZ

JAMES
The 'Old Pretender'.
Born 1688, Died 1766.
Married Clementina Sobieska

ORGE IV   WILLIAM IV   EDWARD – VICTORIA OF SAXE-COBURG

VICTORIA
Born 1819, reigned 1837-1901.

CHARLES
'Bonnie Prince Charlie'
The 'Young Pretender'
Born 1720, Died 1788.

HENRY
Born 1725, Died 1807.
No issue.

ONLY DAUGHTER DIED YOUNG

CHAPTER I

The Early Years

CHARLES EDWARD LOUIS JOHN CASIMIR SILVESTER MARIA, better known throughout history as Bonnie Prince Charlie, was born on the last day of December 1720 in the Palazzo Muti, an old palace which still stands in the Piazzo dei SS Apostoli (the Square of the Holy Apostles) in Rome.

Palazzo Muti

Charles was the son of James Francis Stuart and grandson of James VII of Scotland and II of England. James VII and II was the rightful king, but he was ousted from his throne because of his adherence to the Roman Catholic faith. His daughter Mary had married William of Orange, a prince from the Netherlands. They were both of the Protestant faith, and their supporters invited them to act as regents during James Francis Stuart's minority. He could then be raised as a Protestant and take his rightful place on the throne when he came of age. But William of Orange was not happy with the regency, and demanded the crown.

On 22 January 1689 a vote was taken in Parliament, and the Protestants won by fifteen votes. It was the end of the true royal line of both Scotland and England, but many in these islands, especially in Scotland, still hankered for their true sovereign. These people became known as 'Jacobites', from the Latin for James, 'Jacobus'.

Mary, William of Orange's Queen, died childless in 1694. The ousted King James VII and II died in 1701, and William of Orange the following year. Suddenly it looked like the Stuart star was again in the ascendancy, as James Francis's sister Anne was crowned queen. The Jacobites expected her to push for her brother to be crowned king, especially if she died childless. After all, he was the lawful and legitimate heir.

A huge blow was dealt to the people of Scotland when the Treaty of Union was forced through Parliament on 1 May 1707 against the wish of the vast majority of the people. The Scots had seen their royal line usurped, and now their identity and individuality was being eroded.

Queen Anne died in 1714, and James Francis, who was living in Paris, was regarded by many as the rightful King James VIII of Scotland and III of England. But Parliament intervened again, and it was decided by a majority of one that the crown should be offered to George of the Protestant German House of Hanover. There was consternation amongst the Jacobites in Scotland. On top of every other indignity, this Celtic people had a Saxon ruler imposed upon them. They called King George 'the wee wee German lairdie'.

Several attempts were made to install James Francis on the throne, but for the purpose of this story, the most important event at this time was James's marriage to Princess Clementina Maria Sobieski of Poland. At seventeen, she was one of the wealthiest and most eligible royals in Europe. They were married in 1718. Jacobite hearts beat a little faster when the news of Charles Edward Stuart's birth in Rome was announced at the end of 1720. Bells rang out all over the old city, and the Pope gave a personal blessing to the little prince.

There were English spies in Rome, and soon after the birth the Hanoverian propaganda machine swung into action, the story being spread in London that Charles was born deformed and crippled, and that his mother had had such a terrible time giving birth that she would be unable to bear any more children. Both these stories were later proved to be false, of course; Charles was a healthy child, and four and a half years later his brother Henry Benedict was born.

Just as Charles's father James was called by the Hanoverians 'The Pretender to the Throne', through time Charles would become known as 'The Young Pretender'. His later soubriquet should also be explained – the name Charlie actually comes from Tearlach, the Gaelic for Charles. The pronunciation of Tearlach is very close to the English Charlie, and the Highland pronunciation stuck; this, coupled with the descriptive term, The Bonnie Prince, gives us the name by which he is commonly known today – Bonnie Prince Charlie.

Charles was a direct descendant in blood line from Robert the Bruce, the hero king of Scots. Bruce's daughter, Marjorie, had married his High Steward, Walter, who had fought with distinction at Bannockburn. Their son, who became Robert II of Scotland, was the first of the Stewart dynasty, Stewart being a corruption of Steward. One of the Stewart line was Mary Queen of Scots. She spent much of her childhood in France. The French do not use the letter 'w' and to get round the spelling of Stewart, the variation Stuart came into being. Mary used this version on her return to Scotland.

Lord Inverness reported that Charles 'was as strong and hearty as any porter's child, and runs about everywhere'. He had brownish hair, with golden flecks which caught the sunlight, and eyes of tawny hazel. Charles's brother, Henry Benedict, had softer looks than Charles, with blue eyes and curling blond hair, and he was more studious. Charles was always the more turbulent of the two, but they were close friends as children.

There are many conflicting reports of Charles's demeanour as he was growing up, depending upon whether the speaker was

Jacobite or Hanoverian, and there are snippets that are worth retelling for insights into his character. When he was four, he was walking in one of Rome's gardens with his attendants when they encountered the Pope. At the site of the Pontiff, everyone knelt but Charles who refused to do so. His followers beseeched him, but he could not be made to. By the time he was six and a half, it was reported that he could converse in English, French, Latin and Italian. By this age he also seems to have been a crack shot. He was able to shoot birds off neighbouring roofs with a crossbow, and much to onlookers' surprise, he split a rolling ball with a shaft ten times in succession, proving his aim was no fluke.

Charles's father was very much aware that all that might stand between Charles and the throne was religion. He made sure that Charles was attended by some Protestant advisors. It is possible that James would not have been too averse to his son being reared as a Protestant, but this was shaky ground, as the Stuarts were after all living in Rome, very much dependent on the liberality of the Pope.

Charles's first taste of war came at the age of thirteen, when he was allowed to visit the front line troops at the Siege of Gaeta, where Spanish troops were assailing the Austrians within the town. It was reported that Charles seemed unafraid of the gunfire, and it is said he commented that 'the noise of the cannons was more like music to him than the opera in Rome'.

During his teenage years, Charles was taken to the various cities of Italy – Bologna, Parma, Piacenza, Milan, Venice and Padua. Each tried to outdo the others in giving the most magnificent receptions for him and his small entourage. He was treated as a prince on every occasion, to the disgust of Parliament in London when it heard the tales.

In most of the royal courts of Europe Charles was regarded as rightful heir to the throne of Scotland and England. He would be very aware that the throne should by rights be his, and he would often be making plans for the future. He was surrounded by many loyal exiles, but not all the reports that he received from Jacobite sympathisers travelling from Scotland and England were entirely factual. The level of unrest among the people ready to rise for the Stuarts was sometimes grossly exaggerated.

Certain sections of the French Government were eager for a Stuart restoration across the Channel. With promises of a fleet, well-armed and well-equipped, with perhaps 7,000 soldiers to create a backbone for a landing in England, Charles secretly made his way to Paris. When the French fleet was ready to sail under the command of Marshal Saxe, Charles went to the port of Gravelines, a little east of Calais, the first step to recovering his heritage seemingly now under way.

The fleet set sail in February 1744, but unfortunately the English fleet had knowledge of this undertaking, and moved to intercept. The French fleet managed to avoid a confrontation, due to a deterioration in the weather, and the English lost sight of the French ships, but the weather became so bad that many of them were wrecked on their own coastline at Dunkirk. It was now assumed that the Jacobite threat to England was finished for the forseeable future, but Charles was determined to try and get to Scotland, where he was sure his clansmen would rise for him, even if it meant a solo effort with no backing from France. France indeed pulled out of making another attempt, the stores and munitions from the surviving ships being unloaded and taken away.

As far as Charles was concerned there was now no going back, and with what money he had at his disposal he would hire a ship to take him to Scotland. It took fourteen months of waiting to put everything in order. An armed trading brig, the *du Teillay* was commissioned, along with a man-of-war, the *Elizabeth*, with 500 crew and 64 guns to act as escort on the perilous crossing. They set sail from Nantes on 5 July 1745.

Charles did not inform his father in Rome of his intentions

until the ships were ready to sail, when he sent a messenger to him with a letter. Charles would already have had many adventures in Scotland before his father was appraised of the situation.

On 9 July an English warship, the *Lion*, spotted the two French vessels and came bearing down on the attack. There was much exchange of cannon fire between the two warships, the crew of the *du Teillay*, including Charles, watching from a safe distance. After four hours of continued cannon blasts, the English ship had to sheer off and limp for port. But the very last cannonball fired killed the captain of the French man-of-war, and with many killed and wounded on board, it had to return to the port of Brest. Charles's companions beseeched him to return to French soil, but he would have none of it, and ordered the ship to continue up the western seaboard of England, and on to the Western Isles of Scotland.

Charles was a young man of a strong and wilful disposition, and having come thus far, he was determined to emulate the feats of his illustrious ancestor, Robert the Bruce, and free his rightful kingdom from what he saw as foreign oppression. It was what he was bred to, and he was determined to seize the day.

Bonnie Prince Charlie
A wanted poster issued by the Hanoverians. The text on the poster reads:
'A likeness, notwithstanding the Disguise O yea Any Person who Secures the
Son of the Pretender is Intitled to a Reward of 30,000£.'

Loch Eil

Doune Castle

Hanoverian prisoners being escorted within. Charles passed here on the march south.

Stirling Castle

Bannockburn House

Charles lodged within. It still stands, at Junct on 9 of the M9. The building is a private residence.

Linlithgow Palace

CHAPTER 2

Scotland at Last

THE FIRST SIGHTING CHARLES had of his ancestral homeland was when the *du Teillay* sailed past the little island of Berneray at the southern end of the Outer Isles on 22 July 1745. His heart and mind must have been a confusion of mixed emotions. We can only marvel at his determination to reach Scotland without the expected French aid of men, money and weaponry. I don't imagine for a moment that all that drove him onward was a stubborn conviction that right was on his side. He must have had doubts as to how he would be received, not so much as to whether the Highlanders regarded him as their rightful prince, but more likely over how many would actually be ready to risk all on his behalf. The reality of the situation would be an exuberance of youthful optimism, any dangers in the tasks ahead relegated to the farthest reaches of his mind.

Near the shore of Barra the *du Teillay*'s long boat was launched to make land and see if a guide could be found. By pure luck, the first man encountered was MacNeil of Barra's piper, a staunch Jacobite, who returned to the ship and guided them north to a safe anchorage off the west side of the island of Eriskay. (MAP A1) The Duke of Atholl, on board with Charles, noticed an eagle circling above the ship. He pointed to it, stating 'The king of birds is come to welcome Your Royal Highness upon your arrival in Scotland'.

On 23 July 1745 Charles set foot on Scottish soil for the first time. The rocky bay on Eriskay where he landed, with its strand of beautiful white sand, has ever since been called Coilleag a Phrionnsa – the Prince's Strand. A plant grows there which is referred to by the locals as the Prince's Flower. Legend states that, on stepping ashore, Charles took a handful of seeds from his pocket and scattered them; they grew, and will grow nowhere else in Scotland but on this little island.

Charles's first night in Scotland was spent in the hut of the island's tackman, Angus MacDonald. Angus had no idea of the visitors' identity, and when asked if he had a comfortable bed in his property, he exclaimed that 'it was so good a bed and the sheets were so good, that a prince need not be ashamed to lie in them'. But the bed was not for Charles's use. He installed one of his elderly companions, Sir Thomas Sheridan, in it, and he later took a seat on a pile of turf beside the peat fire and joined in the laughter and banter with the others.

The turf-roofed cabin, or blackhouse as it is known in Scotland, only had a single gap in the rafters to let out the smoke, and much of the peat smoke from the fire hung heavily in the cabin. The Prince had to go out into the stormy night several times in order to clear his eyes and lungs, and Angus MacDonald, inured to the smoke, angrily commented 'What a plague is the matter with that fellow, that he can neither sit or stand still, and neither keep within nor without doors?'. But Charles would surely have been happy to stand out in the dark, in the driving Hebridean rain, glad just to be standing on the soil of Scotland.

The following day a message was sent to Alexander MacDonald, half-brother of Clanranald, one of the MacDonald chiefs, who was living on the island of South Uist to the north of Eriskay. When MacDonald appeared, Charles revealed his identity to him. MacDonald was alarmed that Charles had arrived with only a handful of companions, and advised him to return home to France at once. Charles indignantly replied, 'I am come home, sir, and I will entertain no notion of returning to that place whence I came.'

Charles is often portrayed as some lisping Frenchified dandy, and I feel that some of these comments should help to dispel this myth that is so prevalent in the public imagination. The warlike Gaels accepted him, and many of the snippets of conversation that have survived show him as a man of considerable character. When travelling under an alias, there was nothing effete about him to make onlookers suspicious.

On 25 July the *du Teillay* left Eriskay and sailed across the Minch to Loch nan Uamh (Loch nan OO-ah – Loch of the Caves) (MAP A2). She dropped anchor off Borrodale House. (MAP A3) Summonses were sent out, and several chieftains and various highland gentlemen were rowed out to the ship for an audience with their prince. Like MacDonald earlier, they were alarmed to find that Charles had no French army with him, and expressed doubts about any success for Charles's expedition. He implored the chiefs to reconsider, but they had much to lose, and the failure of the proposed venture to try and regain Charles's father's throne would undoubtedly result in their destruction, so one cannot blame any of them for looking at all aspects of the situation. Suddenly Ranald MacDonald, a brother of Kinlochmoidart, grasped his sword and announced that he would aid Prince Charles, even if no other would draw their sword for him. His enthusiasm spread through the others in the company, and grudgingly, in ones and twos, they began to pledge their word that they would fight for

Borrodale House

9

Charles. It was eventually agreed that the royal standard would be raised in Glenfinnan at the head of Loch Shiel on 19 August, and messengers were sent out to announce this. (MAP A6)

After all the stores on board ship had been offloaded, Charles went ashore on 4 August, staying at Glen Borrodale House from where he wrote letters to other clan chiefs summoning them to the muster at Glenfinnan.

Glen Borrodale House was burnt after Culloden, but it was rebuilt to the original plan using as much of the original materials as possible. The house still stands in this reconstructed condition, a very attractive piece of architecture, totally in fitting with its mountainous surroundings. Charles's bedroom was the attic window farthest right at the front of the house, in his time shadowed by two large trees. There are still a couple of trees in front of the building, but they are somewhat smaller than those in Charles's time.

It was during Charles's stay at Borrodale that Cameron of Locheil pledged allegience to his cause, and it was this act that made many of the other clan leaders climb down from the fence, planting their feet firmly on the Jacobite side.

On Sunday 11 August, Charles and his immediate companions sailed from Loch nan Uamh southwards down the coast to Glenuig Bay in Moidart, where the locals danced a reel on the beach in joy at his arrival. (MAP A4) From there, he and his companions walked the old track up Glen Uig (now traversed by the A861 built in 1966) and down to the sea at Loch Moidart. From here they were rowed up the loch to Kinlochmoidart House in the very heart of Clanranald country. (MAP A5)

Charles stayed at Kinlochmoidart House till the following Thursday, planning his forthcoming campaign. This house was also burnt, like so many others, after Culloden, and was later rebuilt on the same site. It was again rebuilt in a much larger baronial style during the early part of the 20th century. The avenue of giant plane trees dates from before Charles's visit. The walk towards the house from the little church to the west is known locally as the Prince's Walk. Kinlochmoidart House is a private residence and is not open to the public.

Close to the house stand 'The Seven Men of Moidart', seven beech trees in a row in a meadow by the lochside. They were planted to commemorate Charles's seven companions who sailed from France with him, Moidart being seen as the calf country of the '45 rebellion. Only one of the seven, Aeneas MacDonald, was actually born in Moidart. The others were William, the Jacobite Duke of Atholl, four Irishmen – Sir Thomas Sheridan, Charles's old tutor, the Revd George Kelly, Sir John MacDonald, a cavalry officer, and John O'Sullivan, an experienced soldier, and lastly there was Francis Strickland, an English Jacobite.

The beeches are aged and gnarled, one of them dwarf-like compared to the rest. The tree furthest west fell in a storm in 1988 but has been replaced in order to keep the 'Seven' intact. On my last visit during 1999, the easternmost tree was beginning to deteriorate badly, so it may soon need to be replaced. These trees are clearly marked on Ordnance Survey maps, and there is a commemorative cairn and an information board in a lay-by at the side of the adjacent road.

The Seven Men of Moidart

Rumours started to circulate in Scotland that Charles had actually arrived on these shores, and this intelligence eventually reached the ears of General Sir John Cope who was stationed in Edinburgh. Cope was one of the main government soldiers based in Scotland. Taking no chances, Cope ordered two companies of troops stationed at Perth to march north in order to strengthen the garrison at Fort William. These companies (some 100 men) set out on 10 August, reached Fort Augustus at the southern end of Loch Ness on 15 August, and early the following day set out to march down the Great Glen to Fort William.

Highbridge

They had marched the best part of 20 miles and were approaching Highbridge which stands on General Wade's military road a mile or two west of the village of Spean Bridge. (MAP A10) The Redcoat soldiers were just about to cross the bridge which soars high above the tumbling River Spean when bagpipes were heard, and much to the soldiers' alarm, some tartan-clad Highlanders were seen on the bridge brandishing weapons. They then caught glimpses of other men darting about among the rocks on either side. The Redcoat captain sent a sergeant and one man forward to try to ascertain the strength of this 'Highland horde', but two clansmen jumped on them within a few yards and ran the two soldiers at swordpoint over the bridge and out of sight. At that moment shouts went up from the rocks and the bagpipes started to wail again. Panic overtook the two companies of Redcoats and they began to sprint back down the road in the direction of Fort Augustus, terror clutching at their hearts. They would have been surprised to find out that the Highland horde they were fleeing from was in fact eleven men and one piper under the command of Donald MacDonald of Tirnadris. Some of the men had been ordered to dart about between the rocks to alarm the Redcoats, while the others stood on the bridge.

As the Redcoats ran off, another 20 or 30 Highlanders appeared on the scene under the command of Keppoch, a staunch Jacobite. Knowing the Redcoats were following the military road, the Highlanders cut up into Glen Gloy, which runs parallel to the road a little to the east, and came down ahead of them at Laggan at the head of Loch Lochy. The fleeing Redcoats were met with a volley of mus-

Highbridge cairn

ket-fire which killed four and wounded a dozen, whereupon they immediately surrendered. This was the first action of the '45.

The prisoners were taken down Loch Lochy to Achnacarry, and a message was sent to the Governor at Fort William appraising him of the situation, and requesting that he send a surgeon to deal with the Redcoat wounded. The Governor stubbornly refused this request. Cameron of Locheil heard this with incredulity and had the leader of the prisoners, Captain Scott, who had been seriously wounded at Laggan, transported to Fort William so that he could receive the attention he urgently required.

Highbridge plaque

At the little cluster of houses that forms the modern village of Highbridge there is a commemorative cairn erected by the 1745 Association. From this cairn a path runs down to the bridge spanning the gorge of the River Spean. The bridge has deteriorated badly during the last century, the main arch having collapsed into the river far below, and care should be taken on the steep sides of the gorge, especially after rain. Highbridge is sign-posted from the A82, just south of Spean Bridge, and is approached down a single track road.

In a separate incident in the Corrieyairack Pass, four men under the command of MacDonald of Lochgarry captured Captain Switenham of Guise's Regiment as he was making his way to Fort William from the barracks at Ruthven. Captain Switenham was forced to be an eye-witness to the unfurling of the royal standard at Glenfinnan, after which he was allowed to return to England.

Charles meanwhile set out from Kinlochmoidart on Sunday 18 August, accompanied by 50 of the men of Clanranald, to make his way to the appointed meeting at Glenfinnan. They marched a mile or two up Glen Moidart to Brunary, then headed south over the old track to Dalelia on Loch Shiel side. This track is lined with cairns marking the resting places of the funeral parties who came this way for many years, taking their dead down to the shore of Loch Shiel to be rowed over to the old burial ground on Eilean Fhianain – St Finnan's Isle . St Finnan died here in 575 AD and it is from him that Glenfinnan takes its name.

At Dalelia Charles's party embarked and sailed up the loch to Glenaladale where they spent the night. (MAP A7) Today, as then, Glenaladale can only be approached by water or on foot as it lies far from any road.

The party set off again early on the morning of the 19th, the day decreed for the gathering of the clans and the raising of the standard. Between Glenaladale and Glenfinnan, the boats were beached so that everyone could partake of a light meal. The spot where they came ashore has ever since been known as Torr a Phrionnsa (The Prince's Mound). They then sailed for the head of the loch. Charles's heart fell when Glenfinnan came into view. There was no army – in fact, there was no-one in sight apart from a few interested locals and cattle grazing on the heather-covered hillsides. His companions reassured him by pointing out that it was still morning. During the day men did appear in dribs and drabs, but there was no great influx.

Suddenly, at about 4pm, the skirl of bagpipes could be heard in the distance. All eyes turned to see the Camerons of Locheil appear over the hills, some 800 in all, in the full panoply of war. Keppoch then appeared with another 300, and when joined by various MacDonalds and MacGregors, there were some 1,500 men gathered at Glenfinnan. Charles surveyed the scene before him. We can only try to comprehend the pride that must have welled up in him as he looked out over the mass of fighting men, seeing their expectant faces, and they in turn looking at their rightful Prince, the heir of the bloodline of the Ard Righ, or High King of Scots. Neither found fault.

The procedure for the unfurling of the royal banner was immediately set in motion. The banner was blessed by Bishop Hugh MacDonald who was later to be a casualty of Culloden. Duke William of Atholl placed the banner on top of a knoll above the floor of the glen, and there was silence as the banner of the Stuart kings unwrapped itself in the breeze. The cry then went up *'Prionnsa Tearlach Righ nan Ghaidheil'* (Prince Charles, King of the Gael), and the massed Highlanders brandished their basket-hilted broadswords and claymores (*claidheamh-mor* – great sword). After this, Charles gave an eloquent speech about the justice of his father's claim to the throne.

One of the onlookers at the raising of the standard at Glenfinnan was a lady named Jenny Cameron of Glen Dessary, who supplied 200 well-armed Camerons for the Prince's cause. (MAP B28) A false rumour was circulated that Jenny was the Prince's mistress, and there were even caricatures of her in tartan, armed with broadsword and musket, printed in the press of the time.

The following year, a lady was questioned in Edinburgh, and when she gave her name, truthfully, as Jenny Cameron, the

Redcoats believed they had captured the lady they had read about in the press. But it was a case of mistaken identity, as this unfortunate person was an Edinburgh shop owner.

After languishing for several months in Edinburgh Castle, on her release she was inundated with trade when she reopened her haberdashery business, and was rather reluctant to admit to her swelling clientele that she was not the Jenny of dubious fame.

Jenny Cameron's grave

The real Jenny was a staunch Jacobite, and after the '45 she moved to East Kilbride where she lived on a property called Blacklaw. She died there on 27 June 1772 and was buried near her house. (MAP B28) Her grave survives in a children's play area in the middle of the St Leonards housing estate, and the nearby street is named Glen Dessary in honour of her birthplace. Blacklaw was demolished in 1958 and a tree was planted behind her grave in commemoration. Blacklaw was sometimes referred to as Mount Cameron in her memory, and a nearby road is named Mount Cameron Drive.

To mark the raising of the standard there is a monument and a visitor centre at Glenfinnan. The round tower at the lochside surmounted by a statue of a bearded Highlander was erected by Alexander MacDonald of Glenaladale, a descendant of the owner of Glenaladale where Charles stayed the night before the unfurling of the banner. The tower was begun around 1814, but MacDonald did not live long enough to see it completed as he died in Edinburgh on 4 January 1815 at the early age of 28. There are stairs within the tower spiralling to the top where a small hatch gives access to the roof. You can stand up beside the statue of the Highlander, often erroneously referred to as a likeness of Charles, and look out at the tremendous view down Loch Shiel. The parapet, however, is only knee high, and the roof of the tower is not recommended for anyone with a fear of heights. (A small shooting lodge was originally attached to the tower, but it was demolished in Victorian times.)

Glenfinnan Monument

Around the monument three plaques give details of its purpose in Gaelic, Latin and English. The English one states:

> On this spot where Prince Charles Edward first raised his standard, on the 19th August 1745, when he made the daring and romantic attempt to recover a throne lost by the imprudence of his ancestors, this column is erected by Alexander MacDonald Esq. of Glenalladle, to commemorate the generous zeal, the undaunted bravery, and the inviolate fidelity of his forefathers, and the rest of those who fought and bled in that arduous and unfortunate enterprise.

There is some contention as to the exact spot where the standard of the Stuarts was raised. Many books state that 'the monument is built on the site where the banner was unfurled', but this does not seem to be the case. The ground around the monument is particularly boggy, and on my first visit during my schooldays it was much worse than it is now. It would not have been a comfortable place for an army to have gathered. Eye-witness accounts mention a knoll where the standard was raised, and there are also mentions of crossing the River Finnan, on the opposite side to where the monument stands. During the 1980s there was a heather fire in this vicinity and a flat area of rock was laid bare. It was noticed that there were carvings on the face of this rock. As soon as I heard this, I motor-cycled to Glenfinnan and went in search of the rock.

Just a few yards westwards from the visitor centre, the road crosses the River Finnan. Just after the bridge, a road turns northwards under the railway bridge to travel up the glen to Glenfinnan Lodge. This is a private road, but there are a few parking spaces on your right as you turn into the road. Parking here, there is a little path directly opposite which leads between the rhododendron bushes then up the hillside. The carved rock is on the little shoulder above, north of the cottages and before the railway track. An arrow appears to point to the spot where the standard was actually unfurled. There are several Latin inscriptions, including the date and the words 'Caroli Eduardi Stuart', which most likely show the spot where Charles stood.

When I first saw the rock, there were more inscriptions than are now visible. Perhaps the lack of cover has accelerated their deterioration. The Glenfinnan area suffered greatly during the time of the Clearances, so the location of this stone may have simply been lost from local memory when so many of the people left and were scattered.

There are claims for the hill immediately behind the visitor centre as another possible site for the standard, but the carved stone, coupled with the fact that reports mention the crossing of the river, would seem to settle the argument, for me at least.

After Glenfinnan the die was cast. All who had attended knew that, for better or for worse, they were in direct confrontation with the Hanoverian regime. Many of the ordinary clansmen, although sympathetic to Charles's cause, would probably have been much happier staying at home with their families, tending their crops. But the memory of man-rent, a system whereby

Highlanders held tracts of land from their chiefs in return for military service, was still strong. The highland ideal of loyalty was all important, and they had to keep face at all times – if their chieftains asked them to charge into the very jaws of hell, then so be it. All were aware that the first tests of soldiery would not be long in coming.

CHAPTER 3

The March to Edinburgh

ON 21 AUGUST 1745 the Highland army marched eastwards from Glenfinnan, halting at Kinlocheil. (MAP A8) News was brought to Charles that the government in London had issued a proclamation offering a reward of £30,000 for the his capture – a vast sum indeed in those times and the equivalent of many millions today.

Fassiefern House

The army moved onwards down the northern shore of Loch Eil towards the Great Glen, Charles spending the night of 23rd at Fassiefern House. (MAP A9) The Highlanders forded the River Lochy at Moy, and word arrived that an army of Redcoats under the command of General Sir John Cope was heading north towards the government barracks at Fort Augustus on Loch Ness side. Charles's army seethed in anticipation that an early battle might be joined with the Hanoverian forces. At Laggan on Loch Lochy another 700 clansmen came in to swell the ranks. One of them was the noted Coll Ban (Fair Coll), a leader of the men from Knoydart, who stood 6ft 4ins tall and whose strength was legendary throughout the Highlands. A tale told about him was that he once encountered a cow who refused to be driven onto a ferry boat. Coll tried to grasp the cow around the middle but found even his mighty arms were too short for the task. So he removed his bonnet and used it to bridge the gap, and taking a firm grip, lifted the beast from the ground and launched it into the boat.

The army camped that night on the level ground between Loch Lochy and Loch Oich, while Charles, accompanied by his officers, took up quarters at Invergarry Castle, the stronghold of the MacDonnells, a little further up the northern side of Loch Oich. (MAP A11)

The Duke of Cumberland had the castle partially destroyed with dynamite after Culloden because Charles had used it as a place of residence. The gaunt ruins of the castle stand on top of a knoll, named

Invergarry Castle

since time immemorial the Raven's Rock, between the A82 and the lochside. One mile south of the castle at the roadside stands the Well of the Heads. This monument was built in 1812 above the well where in the 1660s a chief took revenge on seven murderers of his people.

Expecting General Cope and his Redcoats to approach from the south via the military road over the Corrieyairack Pass, the army of Highlanders moved to Aberchalder on 27 August, Charles appearing before his men in full highland dress, a sight which much cheered them. (MAP A12) He spent the night in the farmhouse at Aberchalder, and the following morning, the 28th, he led his army of some 1,800 men up into the Corrieyairack, expecting major battle when they encountered General Cope's forces. When the Highlanders reached the high point of the Pass they were astonished to see the countryside laid out before them with no sign of the Redcoats. Many were sorely disappointed. Their martial spirits had been stoked to a white heat and now there was no enemy upon whom to vent their anger. Word eventually came that, rather than risk an encounter Cope and his army, a well-equipped force of some 1,400, had diverted to Inverness.

Charles and his men marched on to spend the night at the little hamlet of Garvamore. Charles stayed at the inn, now demolished, having walked 14 miles with his men that day, no doubt the main topic of conversation being their surprise at Cope's refusal to confront them.

Next day they pushed on to Dalwhinnie, the modern village of that name standing at the side of the A9 just where the hills begin to narrow at the northern end of the Pass of Drumochter. During this march a detachment of some 200 Camerons struck off to the north to attack the government barracks at Ruthven. (MAP A13) There were only twelve men and a sergeant, Terence Mulloy, in residence at Ruthven, and although the Highlanders managed to enter the stable block to pepper the barracks with musket shot, shooting one of the defenders through the head as he looked over the parapet, Mulloy refused to surrender. The Highlanders tried to burn the door down by igniting combustibles piled against it, but this only resulted in one man being killed and two or three wounded. The Camerons soon gave up in disgust and marched off to rejoin the main body.

The barracks at Ruthven survive, complete to the wallhead, just to the east of the A9 at Kingussie. They stand on top of a large

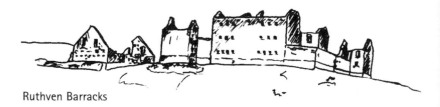

Ruthven Barracks

mound which is partly artificial, having been the site of a large medieval castle built by the Comyn Lords of Badenoch in the 13th century. The castle remains were destroyed when the barracks were built in 1718 to supress the local clans.

On 30 August, after the Camerons who had besieged Ruthven had rejoined the main army, it set off south. In the Highlands topography dictates the routes, and today, driving the A9 through the Drumochter Pass, you are covering the same ground as that walked by the brogans of the Highland host. A halt was made at Dalnacardoch in Atholl, where Charles used the inn (now demolished) as his headquarters for the night.

The following day at 3pm Charles arrived at Blair Castle accompanied by William Duke of Atholl. (MAP A14) William was seeing his heritage for the first time in many years, as his Jacobite sympathies dictated that he had to reside abroad to escape the

Blair Castle

wrath of the Hanoverian authorities. He had left Blair in the hands of his younger brother James who was very much in the pocket of the Hanoverians.

After Charles's arrival, one of the staff at Blair sent a letter to James which stated, 'The Highlanders do not exceed 2,000 in number, two-thirds of whom are the poorest naked-like creatures imaginable. I do not think one half of their guns will fire. Some have guns without swords, and some have swords without guns.' In light of this, it seems incredible that the Highlanders achieved the successes they did against such well-equipped, well-armed and well-drilled regular troops. Many local clansmen enlisted in the Jacobite ranks at Blair – Robertsons, Menzies, Stewarts and Murrays.

Blair Castle is open to the public from April to October each year. There has been a castle on the site for several hundred years, ancient works included in the expanding wings of later eras. The castle's collection of artefacts is a veritable treasure trove for anyone who enjoys Scotland's history.

The Clan Donnachaidh (Robertson) Museum at Bruar, a couple of miles north of Blair Atholl, stands on the ancestral lands of the Robertson family and contains some relics of Charlie and the '45. (MAP A15) The centrepiece must be the Clach na Brataich – the Banner Stone. The Robertsons were always staunch supporters of the royal line of Scotland and fought in every campaign from Bannockburn to Culloden. The Banner Stone appeared during the march to the Battle of Bannockburn. One day the clan standard was stuck into the soil and the Clach na Brataich came to the surface. It is a circular ball of crystal a couple of inches in diameter, similar to the one on top of the sceptre in the Scottish Crown Jewels. The Robertsons carried this stone into every battle from Bannockburn on. It was said the hue of light which emanated from the crystal foretold the outcome of the fight to come.

As Bonnie Prince Charlie was a direct descendent of the mighty Bruce, the Robertsons have a formidable legacy of loyalty to the rightful heirs of Scotland that few can match. Long may their little museum stand on the last remnants of their once extensive clan territories.

While at Blair, Charles is said to have dined at nearby Lude House which is privately owned and not open to the public.

On 3 September the army moved on, threading through the Pass of Killiecrankie where in earlier days an army fighting for William of Orange was destroyed by a Jacobite army of Highlanders led by 'Bonnie Dundee' who unfortunately was killed at the battle. The site of the battle must have been an inspiration to Charles's army, many of them the sons and grandsons of the men who had fought here 56 years earlier.

On arriving at Dunkeld, Charles made his headquarters at Dunkeld House which was destroyed sometime around 1830. While Charles stayed here, Cameron of Locheil with a detachment of his clansmen marched on to Perth and took it in the name of the Stewart kings.

The following day Charles left Dunkeld, stopping to dine at Nairne House near Auchtergarven before heading on to Perth. Nairne House was sadly demolished in 1759 – it was said to be a magnificent mansion, containing no less than 365 windows.

When Charles entered Perth, crowds lined the streets hoping to catch a glimpse of the rightful heir to the Scottish throne, the recipient of the blood of the ancient line of kings. (MAP A16) He did not disappoint them, riding into the city dressed in tartan. He took up quarters in an inn which is in use to this day, the Salutation Hotel in South Street. This fine old building has a brass plaque on its front wall proclaiming its association with Prince Charles. The room which Charles occupied is still in use as a bedroom.

Salutation Hotel, Perth

Many local gentry came to Perth to offer their services to the Jacobite cause, the most important being Lord George Murray, a brother of the Duke of

Atholl, who was an experienced soldier and whose influence on the campaign was to have great effect.

Lord George Murray was born in 1705. At the age of ten he had taken a small part in the Jacobite rising of 1715. In the rising of 1719 he and his brother William fought in the Battle of Glen Shiel. Lord George, only fourteen, was wounded in this unsuccessful fight. Fleeing Scotland, he became an officer in the Sardinian army, becoming a master of tactics and strategy. He was eventually pardoned by George I and returned to Scotland, and took part in Jacobite intrigues both in Scotland and in London. He was a tall, robust man and a natural leader. He did not suffer fools gladly, was contemptuous of those who did not meet his high standards, and was seen by some as arrogant, but a soldier of such experience must have been a welcome addition to the ranks of the Jacobite army.

While Charles was at Perth, he is said to have visited Scone Palace, in the grounds of which is the traditional crowning place of the monarchs of Scotland. (MAP A17) It would have raised many emotions in Charles to have stood on this hallowed spot, reflecting on the scores of his ancestors who had received the gold circlet of Scotland upon their brow while seated on the Stone of Destiny.

Charles also attended Protestant church services in Perth, hoping he could instil a religious tolerance in his people.

Balhaldie House, Dunblane

On 11 September the Highland army struck its camp on the North Inch near Perth and resumed the march south towards Edinburgh. They travelled by way of Gask, then followed the line of the A9 through Auchterarder, their destination that night being Dunblane. (MAP A18) The army bivouaced at the park of Keir which lies beside the round-about at Junction 11 on the m9, just south of Dunblane. Charles spent the nights of 11 and 12 September at Balhaldie House which still stands, gable on to the upper part of Dunblane High Street at the junction with Smithy Loan. It is a private residence and has a little plaque on its gable wall announcing its Charlie connection.

On the morning of the 13th Charles and his army moved a little north-westward to the village of Doune which is overshadowed by its mighty medieval castle. (MAP A19) At the time of the '45 Doune was a famous centre for gun-making. Doune pistols are much sought after today. It is reported that the first shot fired in the American War of Independence was from a Doune pistol.

Balhaldie House plaque

Entering Doune by the road from Dunblane there is a pair of large gates and a wall on the left. This is the boundary of Newton House. Although it was early morning, all of Doune was astir to see the spectacle of the Highland army marching through. The wall of Newton House provided a grandstand for several young ladies connected to the property. They asked Charles to enter the house for some refreshment. He regretfully declined, but one of the ladies offered him a glass of wine, and Charles raised it to his lips, drinking the health of the ladies. Another young

Newton House

lady, Clementina Edmonstoun, was determined to go further. She ran up as Charles prepared to ride on, asking permission to 'pree his Royal Highness's mou'. This expression in broad Scots had to be translated by one of the Prince's companions. Charles, laughing, leaned from his horse and lifted the girl bodily from the ground, planting kisses on her face.

From Doune, the army marched to the River Forth, crossing at the Bridge of Frew. (MAP A20) The bridge is now demolished, but

Fords of Frew

there are remants of its stonework on both banks of the river. Some accounts mention the army crossing the Forth by the Fords of Frew which lie just a few yards downstream from the remains of the bridge, but as it appears the bridge was in existence in 1745, it would be strange if the army elected to get a soaking when the bridge was nearby.

A tale exists that the Highlanders forced some of the local farmers to join their route of march, bringing their horses and carts with them to carry the army provisions. When the carts were unhitched for the night south of the Forth, the farmers decided to make a break for it, taking their horses but leaving their carts behind. They knew the bridge would be guarded, and so galloped into the river to try to make a crossing. Unfortunately, the bank at the far side was too high for the horses to clamber out, and they were swept some distance downstream before a place was found where the banks were low enough for them to effect their escape.

Once everyone had successfully crossed the barrier of the Forth, Charles and his officers were given refreshments at Leckie House, or as it is more popularly called today, Old Leckie. (MAP A21) It stands about a mile south-east of the crossing at Frew, south of the A811, some six miles west of Stirling. It is a private residence, but its roofs and chimneys can be glimpsed through the surrounding trees from the road.

Old Leckie

A rumour had been spread that the Jacobite army's advance was destined to take them to Glasgow. As this city was now only 20 miles away across the Gargunnock and Campsie Hills, which would be little barrier to the Highlanders, Hanoverian officers readily believed Glasgow to be their destination, but the Highlanders pushed on to Touch House, further east and only a mile or two from Stirling itself. Touch House, which is privately owned, stands not far from the village of Cambusbarron.

Next morning, Saturday 14 September, they resumed their march in the direction of Edinburgh, going through St Ninians, on the line of the modern main road from Stirling to Edinburgh. (MAP B1) Seeing the royal banner carried alongside Charles, the gunners at Stirling Castle used it as a target and fired several shots. Although a couple fell close to the banner, no damage was done. A halt for food was taken on the battlefield at Bannockburn, and we can be sure that many of the Highlanders looked around them curiously at the scene where their ancestors had helped Charles's

Bannockburn House

ancestor, King Robert the Bruce, to win Scotland's greatest ever victory against England.

Charles went to Bannockburn House which still stands complete with some later additions between the M9 and the A91 Bannockburn turnoff, beside the large roundabout that forms Junction 9 of the M9. (MAP B2) News was brought to him that a party of dragoons under the Hanoverian Colonel Gardiner was stationed ahead at Linlithgow, and so a push forward was immediately called for. A halt was made for the night at Callendar House near Falkirk, where Charles spent the night, his army camping in the fields to the east of the house. (MAP B3) Callendar House was originally a tower house but was extended over the years to form a large mansion. Its exterior has not changed greatly since 1745 and it is now a museum open to the public.

Charles learnt that the Hanoverians were encamped a little west of Linlithgow on the far side of the bridge over the River Avon. He gave orders to have 1,000 men secretly assembled and made a pretence of retiring to bed to throw off the scent those around him at who may have had Hanoverian sympathies. He crept out of a back door of the house in the middle of the night and with Lord George Murray led the Highlanders on an attack. They decided to cross the ford over the Avon a mile and a half upstream from the bridge and attack Gardiner in the rear. But on approaching the Avon, it was discovered that Gardiner, alarmed at the sudden nearness of Charles's army, had retired to Coltness near Edinburgh. Disappointed at the failure to bring the enemy to battle, Charles marched his men forward into the town of Linlithgow where he visited Linlithgow Palace, the home of his Stuart ancestors. (MAP B4) The old fountain in the courtyard ran with wine to mark the event. Once the rest of the army arrived from Falkirk, they moved on a few miles further east to Kincavil where they spent the night, most of the officers sleeping with their men in the fields in their plaids. Early next morning they continued towards Edinburgh. Their route took them through Winchburgh

Gray's Mill, Slateford plaque

and Corstorphine, where Charles sent off a deputation to Edinburgh to call for the city to be handed over to the rightful heir, then they moved a little south to Slateford. Camp was made beside the Water of Leith and a little-known plaque marks the spot. (MAP B5) It is attached to the underside of the concrete bridge carrying the Union Canal over Slateford Road and states that 'Charles's army was encamped near this spot'.

Charles lodged within Gray's Mill, a few hundred yards downstream on the left bank. This mill stood into the 20th century but disappeared when Slateford became more and more industrialised. Its site on the riverbank is covered by Bookers Cash & Carry warehouse. Its name, however, lives on in Graysmill School which stands a little further east of the original site. A good viewpoint for scanning the terrain is on the aqueduct which carries the Union Canal over the Water of Leith. It is easily accessible from the bridge which bears the commemorative plaque.

Meanwhile, in Edinburgh, a Brigadier Fowkes had arrived from London to command two regiments of cavalry. These united with Colonel Gardiner's men who had prudently retired from the bridge over the Avon. They marched out to defend the city from the Jacobite threat, but when they encountered a small group of Highlanders who peppered them with musket shot, the front ranks of the Hanoverians broke and ran back through the rest of the army, shouting that they were being attacked. The panic spread, and all the Hanoverian forces were soon in flight. The bemused townsfolk of Edinburgh, high on the ridge of the Castle Rock, watched as terrified cavalrymen urged their horses along the Lang Dykes, a lane which today is covered by George Street in the New Town to the north of the Castle. They did not stop till they reached Musselburgh. The shameful flight along the Lang Dykes soon came to be known derisively in Scotland as the 'Canter of Coltbrig'. The Hanoverians had run from only a handful of Charles's men, the rest of the Highland army still encamped at Slateford.

On 17 September Cameron of Locheil marched his Highlanders under cover of darkness close to the walls of Edinburgh and they quietly took up positions near the gate at Netherbow Port. Just as the first traces of dawn began to lighten the eastern sky, the gate was opened to

Holyroodhouse

let out a nobleman's coach. Seizing their chance, the Highlanders stormed the gate and overpowered the guard. Detachments spread out through the city, and the first most inhabitants knew of the change of garrison was when they rose in the morning to find tartan-clad soldiers in the streets. There is a famous anecdote about one citizen, who was taking his morning walk, coming across a Highlander sitting astride a cannon. He said to the Highlander, 'Surely you are not the same troops who were mounting guard yesterday?' To which the Highlander replied, 'Och no – they've been relieved.' At the east end of the castle esplanade in Edinburgh, stands a building known as Cannonball House due to the fact that there is what appears to be a cannonball embedded in the wall, local legend stating that the shot was fired from one of the castle's cannon during the '45. It is, in fact, a device to show the maximum water level in the former reservoir opposite.

Word was brought to Charles at Gray's Mill of the 'taking' of Edinburgh, and he marched the rest of the army on a south-about route to the hill near the ruins of St Anthony's Chapel, where he could look down on his ancestral home of Holyroodhouse and the remains of Holyrood Abbey, where several of his ancestors were buried. Many of the men made camp in Hunter's Bog, between Salisbury Crags and Arthur's Seat. Charles himself rode down and through the gates of Holyrood. Edinburgh was once more in the hands of the Stuarts. (MAP B6)

CHAPTER 4

Prestonpans

I HAVE HEARD IT SAID that Bonnie Prince Charlie should have stayed put once he had control of Scotland. Part of me feels he should have done so, but I don't believe for a minute that England would have let the matter rest. After all, there are and always have been ten Englishmen for every Scot, and I do not think they would have been long in asserting their superiority. It was assumed, too, that the English Jacobites would rise en masse once Charles crossed the border and set out to regain his father's throne, which meant the crown of the United Kingdom, not just that of the ancient northern realm. It is interesting to speculate on what would have happened with one royal house ruling Scotland from Edinburgh, and another ruling England from London, some 140 years after the Union of the Crowns.

While Charles was at Holyrood, his father was proclaimed James III and VIII at the Mercat Cross of Edinburgh which in 1745 stood in the middle of the High Street a little east of Parliament Close. Crowds thronged the streets, many wearing the White Cockade, a little white knot symbolising the white rose of Scotland – the badge of the Jacobites.

Most of Charles's army would never have been south of the highland line, and the Highlanders, used to the immense skies and panoramas of hills and glens, must have been bemused by the narrow closes and thronging populace of the city of Edinburgh. A spy for the Hanoverians sent a report to General Cope, giving an account of the Highlanders encamped upon Arthur's Seat. He reported: 'They were for the most part strong, active, and hardy men, but were of a very ordinary size, and if clothed like low-countrymen, they would appear inferior to King George's troops, but the highland garb favoured them very much, as it showed their naked limbs, which were very strong and muscular, and their stern countenances and bushy uncombed hair gave them a fierce, barbarous and imposing aspect.' He also reported on their weaponry, and mentioned how some carried swords but no guns, and vice versa. He also made mention of some soldiers carrying Lochaber axes. These comprised a shaft usually seven to ten feet long, with a wicked curving blade, like the blade of a scythe, attached at one end. It could either be swung or used in a chopping motion.

Intelligence was received of the landing at Dunbar, east of Edinburgh, by General Cope and his army. They had sailed from Aberdeen on 15 September, arriving at Dunbar on the 17th. The Jacobite army, in response, moved from their camp at Hunter's Bog and took up new quarters at the village of Duddingston which lies in the shadow of Arthur's Seat.

Cope met up with the troops who had taken part in the Canter of Coltbrig and they helped to swell his ranks. He moved westwards on 10 September to Haddington, and on hearing this, Charles left Holyrood and joined his army at Duddingston. (MAP B7) Charles and his Highlanders relished the chance to bring Cope to battle. A council of war was held in the building requisitioned as Charles's headquarters in Duddingston. It stands in the road named The Causeway and has a little inscribed stone above its front door which states, 'Here Prince Charles held his Council of War before Prestonpans, 19th Sep. 1745'.

Duddingston

35

I am always a little envious of people lucky enough to stay in such a property that has so much history attached. Many times during my travels assembling information for this book I would mention to people in shops, hotels, etc – anywhere where Charles had stayed – that it must be a bonus working in an establishment like that, casting one's mind back to the days when the son of the rightful Stuart king dwelt within the same stone walls that have survived to this day. In some places the residents had no idea of the royal connection. In others people were very proud, and knew every detail of the circumstances involved.

in this house on 19th September 1745 PRINCE CHARLES EDWARD STUART held his Council of War before the battle of Prestonpans

Duddingston plaque

After spending the night at Duddingston, Charles awoke on the morning of the 20th and readied himself to lead his men against the forces under Cope. At about 9 am, he appeared before his army and drew his broadsword, exclaiming, 'Gentlemen, I have flung away the scabbard, with God's assistance I don't doubt of making you a free and happy people. Mr Cope shall not escape us as he did in the Highlands.' The advance was given and the stern countenances of the Highlanders lit up in smiles when one of their number raised aloft a broom on a pole, a sign that they were going to sweep the enemy into the Firth of Forth.

They made their way speedily to Musselburgh and crossed the River Esk by what is known as the Roman Bridge. (MAP B8) This old bridge stands on the Esk in the town centre, a little upstream from the busy modern road bridge. It is called the Roman Bridge due to the belief that a structure has existed here since Roman times. The bridge looks medieval and it was certainly the scene of some action during the Battle of Pinkie in 1547, when Scottish soldiers including the Earl of Montrose were killed on the bridge by a shot from an English vessel lying in the Firth of Forth off

Musselburgh. The bridge was on the only route from Edinburgh to the south-east and the border, and it must have seen many great names from Scotland's history making their way over its ancient cobbles.

Roman Bridge, Musselburgh

Word was brought to Cope that the Jacobites were on the south side of the Esk, and he pushed his men forward towards Prestonpans to intercept. The Highlanders reached the hill at Fawside about noon, and from this viewpoint they could see Cope's men drawn up at Preston Grange. They proceeded in the direction of the village of Tranent. At first sight it looked as if the Redcoats had made a grave mistake in their choice of position, but closer analysis of the terrain proved that there was a large stretch of very soft and marshy ground between Tranent and Prestonpans which protected the Hanoverian flanks. There was some jockeying for position on both sides, the armies evenly matched in numbers at least, each comprising some 2,500 men, but the day was growing late and the sun was beginning to sink in the west. It became obvious that it would be the next day before any major confrontation took place, although 50 Camerons who had taken up positions in the churchyard at Tranent were within range of the Hanoverian cannon and had to withstand some heavy gunfire across the bog. The church is still standing, overlooking the site of the Hanoverian positions.

The Jacobite army made its way a little east of the village to camp for the night. Word was brought to Charles that there was a possible route over the swampy ground that could be crossed by determined men. The Highlanders, by their very nature, were ideally suited to try this. At 3am the army was roused and every man told to make ready. The Highlanders from their slightly higher position

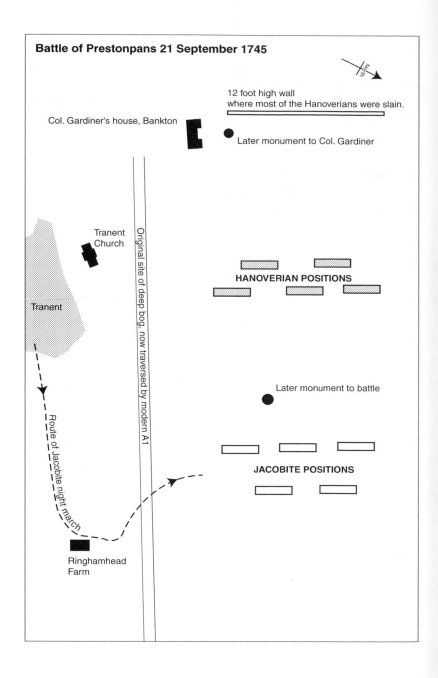

Battle of Prestonpans 21 September 1745

North

12 foot high wall
where most of the Hanoverians were slain.

Col. Gardiner's house, Bankton

Later monument to Col. Gardiner

Tranent
Church

Original site of deep bog, now traversed by modern A1

HANOVERIAN POSITIONS

Tranent

Later monument to battle

Route of Jacobite night march

JACOBITE POSITIONS

Ringhamhead
Farm

were able to look over the bog and scan the fires of the enemy camp. They made their way over the farm of Ringhamhead, then swung north, crossing the worst of the swampy ground and negotiating a water-filled ditch, which Charles almost fell into, before appearing at the eastern side of the enemy. The gap between the two armies at Tranent and Prestonpans is today traversed by the main route (the A1) from Edinburgh to the south. It crosses the site of the bog which has been drained, so it is not now possible to walk the route that the Highlanders took to surprise the Hanoverian army.

As the Highlanders lined up to prepare for battle, a cannon-shot was fired in warning as somebody in the Hanoverian lines woke up to what was happening. Another shot was fired, and one of Locheil's Camerons was hit in the legs by the cannonball. His scream of pain acted as a signal to the entire Highland army, and as one unit they launched into a full charge. The Highland charge would have been a terrifying prospect for any man to face. There were no tactics involved, it was just pure aggression, brute force and slashing weapons – a determination to break right through the enemy lines. The redcoated Hanoverian soldiers watched the wave of tartan come on at the run. One or two shots were fired, then most of these regular, well-trained and well-armed soldiers decided that they would rather be elsewhere. But the tartan tide was upon them, screaming their clan war cries. From the first charge until the battle's end took only a few minutes. Of the 2,500 Redcoats, 500 were slaughtered by the claymores and Lochaber axes of the Highlanders. Eye-witness accounts say that the battlefield was littered with hands, arms and legs, and even noses and other facial features were strewn on the grass. Fourteen hundred were taken prisoner, and 900 of these had cut wounds of one kind or another. The other 600 or so managed to flee to safety, including Cope, who eventually reached the sanctity of Berwick. The losses on the Jacobite side were between 30 and 40. The Hanoverian forces weren't just outflanked by the Jacobites. To their rear was the 12 foot high wall marking the boundary of part of Lord Grange's property. As can be imagined, this barrier seriously hampered the fleeing Redcoats ability to escape the slashing weaponry of the Jacobite forces. Many of the Hanoverians were killed here as a result.

One of the Hanoverian officers, Colonel Gardiner, by a strange quirk of fate, actually lived in Prestonpans. He was felled by a blow from a Lochaber axe, close to his own garden. (MAP B9) There is some debate as to whether he died on the battlefield or

was carried to the manse close to Tranent church where he finally gave up the ghost. He was buried at the west end of the old church, but no tombstone marks his grave which is now under later church buildings.

Bankton, Colonel Gardiner's house

His house, Bankton, stands a little south-east of the railway station. It is in a beautiful state of preservation. I remember seeing Bankton House in the early 1980s, when it was lying derelict, having been badly burnt during the 1960s. It has since been restored and is now a private residence. Directly in front of the house, beside the railway line, is a monument to Colonel Gardiner, created in 1853 by Archibald Ritchie, an Edinburgh sculptor. It can be reached by crossing the bridge over the railway line at the station. When exiting the station to the south, there is a little gap in the wall on your immediate left. A path leads the few hundred yards to the monument.

Another Hanoverian officer killed at Prestonpans was Captain Stewart of Physgill. An article written about him in the 1890s mentions 'he was buried in the churchyard of Prestonpans, and over his grave is an interesting memorial tablet, although it is partially weather-worn'. I scoured the graveyard 100 years after this account was written but could find no trace of the gravestone. Some of the memorials in the churchyard are so weather-worn that no inscriptions remain, so perhaps one of these is Captain Stewart's, time having obliterated the 'interesting memorial'.

From the station, driving due east, you reach the monument to the battle, a simple squat stone edifice bearing the date 1745. It stands at a junction, and if you turn right here and drive towards the A1, you will notice a grass pyramid. It is a vast structure and has a path to the summit at each corner. The summit has sign boards and markers showing how the Battle of Prestonpans was fought. It is an excellent viewpoint, with all the main positions laid out before you and the church and village of Tranent directly behind.

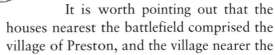

Cairn at Prestonpans

It is worth pointing out that the houses nearest the battlefield comprised the village of Preston, and the village nearer the shore is called Prestonpans – derived from the huge commercial salt pans in the area. The name Prestonpans is used today for the entire built-up area and was adopted for the name of the battle, although the Highlanders directly afterwards referred to it as the Battle of Gladsmuir.

While in this vicinity it is worth taking a look at Hamilton House and Northfield House, two old baronial houses in Preston which existed at the time of the battle. The Mercat Cross, erected in 1617, still stands, but even older are the remains of lofty Preston Tower, a fortified tower house owned by the Hamiltons and abandoned in 1663. Nearby in its now landscaped grounds is a dovecot. So much history, all crammed into one little area.

On the eve of the battle Cope is said to have used a house in

Cockenzie for his sleeping quarters. This building was familiarly called 'The Ink Bottle' due to its shape. Enquiries in the Cockenzie area regarding this structure drew a blank and I can only assume that it has long since been demolished.

Some anecdotes about Prestonpans have survived. One of the Highlanders is said to have taken a gold pocket watch from the body of a Redcoat officer. The need to know the time was not a priority for the average clansman, and a pocket-watch was a rare item north of the Highland Line. The Highlander carried it for several days till it stopped ticking, whereupon he offered it to a passer-by with the comment 'The beastie is dead!'

Probably the best known and most enduring legacy of the battle itself is the familiar song and pipe tune 'Hey, Johnnie Cope!'. Cope has gone down in history in song, although not as the victor in a battle which, logistically at least, should have been been won by the forces of King George.

CHAPTER 5

The March South from Edinburgh (Edinburgh to Carlisle)

AFTER PRESTONPANS WAS FOUGHT AND WON, Charles gave orders that all the Hanoverian wounded were to be tended and their wounds dressed. He then rode off to Musselburgh where he spent the night of 21 September at Pinkie House, while the army quartered in Musselburgh. Pinkie House stands at the east end of the High Street. Its oldest tower is said to date back to 1390, but later building work dates from 1613. It is especially famous for its 80-foot long gallery with its magnificent painted ceiling. The house is now part of Loretto School.

News of the victory arrived in Edinburgh only three hours after the battle when a party of Camerons appeared, pipes playing, carrying some of the Hanoverian flags. The next day the whole army returned, the victorious Highlanders firing muskets into the air in celebration. One lady, watching from a balcony, was grazed by a bullet, and in later years she recounted the story to Sir Walter Scott. She said that it was lucky she was a Jacobite, because if she had been a Hanoverian, people might have thought it was deliberate.

Charles took no part in the celebrations and banned the burning of bonfires because he did not wish to rejoice over the deaths of so many who, after all, were his own subjects, although perhaps misguided as to their loyalty.

While recruitment took place to enlist more men from the Highlands, Charles spent the next few weeks at Holyrood, speaking with his council and attending balls. An interesting report made by a Hanoverian spy to London runs, 'The young Chevalier is about five feet eleven inches high, very proportionably made, wears his own hair, has a full forehead, a small but lively eye, a round brown complexioned face, nose and mouth pretty small, full under the chin, not a long neck, under his jaw a pretty many pimples. He is always in highland habit, as are all about him. He had his boots on, as he always has.'

During October, the Jacobite army swelled to twice the size it had been at the Battle of Presonpans. Many Highlanders, en route to Edinburgh, were ferried across the Forth from Alloa to Elphinstone so that they would be out of range of the guns from the hostile garrison at Stirling Castle. Although many lowland Scots had now enlisted in the ranks of Charles's army, for the sake of uniformity they all dressed in the tartan plaid of the Gael.

The army set off from Edinburgh for Dalkeith where they camped on the ground between the Melville Burn and Newbattle Water. Dalkeith has played a major part in every era of Scotland's story since the time of David 1. Charles spent two days at the Palace at Dalkeith. The Palace stands on the north side of Dalkeith on the ground before the meeting of the North and South Esk rivers. It was constructed around 1700, although there had been a fortification on the site since the 1100s. The parks of the Palace, some 1,035 acres, are ringed by an impressive stone wall which must have cost a vast sum to build, and the house itself is filled with treasures which must have needed great riches to amass. During the 1st and 2nd November preparations were made for the long march south into England, to culminate hopefully in London where the House of Stuart would again form the ruling dynasty.

Sunday 3 November saw the start of this great adventure, the army splitting into two lines of march, with Charles leading the eastern column and the Dukes of Atholl and Perth leading the western. Charles's route took him through Pathhead and the pass over the Lammermuir Hills at Soutra. Soutra has seen around 80 full scale armies of invasion from England in its time, but in this instance it saw one from Scotland that would reach further south than any that had gone before.

Charles halted the first night at Lauder and rested in Thirlstane Castle, an imposing structure dating originally from 1595. (MAP B10) Going south from Lauder on the A68, the A697 branches off east, and the entrance to the castle grounds is some 700 yards down this road. The castle is open to the public at certain times.

Charles heard the following morning that the rearguard of the army had halted at Channelkirk, a good six or seven miles north of Lauder. He insisted on riding back and personally leading them forward before continuing the general advance. During times of march, Charles constantly checked up and down the columns of men, fussing over them like a hen over her chicks to make sure there were no stragglers. One of his officers, Murray of Broughton, spoke later of the 'Prince's untiring attention to his military duties'.

That night's goal was Kelso, which was reached on the evening of the 4th, and Charles lodged at Sunlaws, a house about four miles out of town on the Jedburgh road. (MAP B11) The Prince's quarters were in the wing to the right of the central tower. It was a property of the famous border family of Kerr, and was restored after a bad fire in 1885. Sunlaws is now a hotel whose grounds form the only championship golf course in the Borders.

There is one little momento in Kelso itself that is said to stem from the passage of the Jacobite army through the town. In Roxburgh Street there is the mark of a horseshoe in one of the cobbles of the road. It is reported that Charles's horse cast a shoe on this spot as he rode amongst his men on the journey south.

Charles remained at Sunlaws until the morning of the 6th while cavalry units were sent out across the south-east of Scotland to confuse the Hanoverians as to the Jacobites' objective. Charles wished to keep them guessing. Would it be Newcastle, Carlisle, or somewhere else? Lord George Murray, in command of one of the units, made a feint in the direction of Berwick, before he forded the Tweed west of Coldstream. The Highlanders, somewhat surprisingly, did not like the look of the river as it was running very high, and Lord George himself crossed the river and danced at the far side to show there was no danger. His men splashed in, and once everyone was safely across they made their way to Jedburgh to meet up with Charles who had gone there from Sunlaws. In Jedburgh Charles slept at the Upper Nags Head Inn, 13 Castlegate, which was demolished in 1899 to make way for a new public library. (MAP B12)

Continuing the march in a south-westerly direction, Charles spent the 7th at Larriston, then on Friday 8th, after a march of 13 miles, the army came to the banks of the River Esk at Gritmill near Canonbie. (MAP B13) Charles crossed the Esk and set foot on English soil for the first time. Murray of Broughton reported, 'It was remarkable that this being the first time they entered England, the Highlanders, without any orders being given, all drew their swords with one consent upon entering the river, and every man as he landed on the other side, wheeled about to the left and faced Scotland again.' Perhaps the psyche of the Scots has not changed too greatly over the centuries. Often, driving home to Sotland from long trips south, I see that wee blue sign on the M74 which says 'Welcome to Scotland', and no matter how wet and cold I am, or whether I have been absent for a day or a month, my heart lifts at the very sight of it!

The night after the river crossing into England Charles spent in the village of Riddings at the house of a Mr David Murray. The march resumed next morning, the army passing through the village of Longtown, then crossing the route of the modern M6, arriving in Rockcliffe on the banks of the River Eden. Here they were re-united with the troops under the command of the Duke of

Atholl and the Duke of Perth who had taken the more westerly route, travelling from Dalkeith through Peebles, Broughton, Moffat and Lockerbie, before crossing the Esk near Gretna and going on to Rockcliffe. The whole army crossed the River Eden at about 2pm.

History has a strange way of twisting and turning. From Rockcliffe, as the crow flies, it is only a short hop along the Solway shore to the monument which commemorates the spot where Edward I of England, or Longshanks as he was known, breathed his last, fighting to the end to subjugate Scotland. Charles was not only a direct descendent of King Robert the Bruce, but also had Edward's blood running in his veins. Longshanks was the great enemy of William Wallace. Wallace was a vassal of the High Steward of Scotland, the Stewards being based in the Renfrew area. Wallace was born at Elderslie on their lands. The Stewards of Scotland became the reigning family of Scotland after marrying into the House of Bruce, and their descendent was now leading his gallant Highlanders onto English soil.

The Eden was forded just south of Rockcliffe and at Cargo, a little upstream. The Jacobites took up quarters in the various farms and communities scattered to the west of Carlisle. Charles lodged in the village of Moorhouse, on the B5307 which runs west from Carlisle. (MAP B14) While at Moorhouse, some of Charles's officers discovered a child hidden in a house. The child's mother began to scream, much to the consternation of the Highlanders present. It turned out that a rumour had been spread abroad that Highlanders ate children, and so the woman had made an effort to conceal hers!

The following day, Sunday 10 November, a formal demand for the surrender of Carlisle 'within two hours' was delivered by a man named Robinson. (MAP B15) The Carlisle magistrates promptly arrested this unfortunate individual, and decided the best policy would be to lock the gates and do nothing, except to fire a few cannonballs. It was a foggy day, and the Highland regiments made the best of this cover and moved closer to the city walls. Charles accompanied one of his divisions to the south side of the city where he made Black Hall his quarters. (MAP B16)

The next morning, the entire Jacobite army was marched eastwards away from Carlisle. Information had been received that Marshal Wade, commanding a large Hanoverian army, was making his way westwards from Newcastle to relieve Carlisle. Charles was happy to try to intercept Wade and bring him to battle if possible – spirits must still have been high after

Shoe shop in Brampton

the resounding victory at Prestonpans. The army halted in the vicinity of Brampton, some ten miles or so east-north-east of Carlisle, in slightly hilly country which was deemed suitable for the highland way of fighting. Charles made his headquarters in a house in High Cross Street in the very centre of Brampton. (MAP B17) This little building, dating from 1603, is still in beautiful condition and is currently in use as a shoe shop. It has a little oval plaque on its wall testifying to its connection with Charles.

PRINCE CHARLIE'S HOUSE

THIS BUILDING
DATES FROM THE YEAR 1603.

IN 1745 'BONNIE' PRINCE CHARLIE
ESTABLISHED HIS HEADQUARTERS HERE
DURING THE SIEGE OF CARLISLE ON
NOVEMBER 12th TO 18th 1745.

Brampton plaque

If you are in Brampton to take a look at the building in High Cross Street, there is another memorial of these times nearby. Taking Gelt Road which runs south from the town centre, going uphill, turn right into Capon Tree Road. Following this leafy residential street west, you come to a bend where the old route has been superceded by a new one. In the little cul-de-sac that remains of the old road, on the left beneath the trees is a touching memorial. The inscription reads: 'This Stone is placed to mark the site of the ancient Capon Tree under whose shade the judges of assize rested and upon whose branches were executed October XXI MDCCXLVI for adherence to the cause of the Royal Line of Stewart Colonel James Innes, Captain Patrick Lindesay, Ronald MacDonald, Thomas Park, Peter Taylor, Michael Delard. These six men were executed here in 1746 for supporting Charles's cause.' As they were led here they would have been able to see the rolling border hills of Scotland to the north. It is the discovery of such poignant reminders of the past, sad though so many of these are, that make my love affair with the history of Scotland so worthwhile.

Capon Tree, Brampton

The following day, various scouts and outriders having returned to Brampton with the news that the Hanoverian army under Wade was nowhere to be seen and that the advance from Newcastle was a myth, it was decided that half of the army would return to the siege of Carlisle while Charles remained at Brampton with the rest. Charles escorted the army as far as the village of Warwick, however, where he dined in the Oak Parlour in Warwick Hall.

Earthworks were raised at Carlisle in readiness for the siege, the Highlanders working steadily through the day. At 3pm a despatch rider arrived from Wade at Newcastle with a message stating that he would not be able to relieve the citizens of Carlisle from the threat of Charles's forces. By the following morning, the news that relief was not coming had spread through the garrison at Carlisle, and with the Jacobite army surrounding the city, the defenders threw down their weapons. Seeing the situation as hopeless, the magistrates of Carlisle raised a white flag above the city.

Word of the surrender was conveyed to a surprised Charles at Brampton, and the following morning, Friday 15 November, his forces took control of Carlisle. Charles had lost only one man during the taking of Carlisle, an Irish officer named Calton. He was

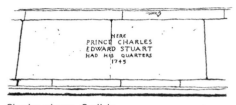

working on the earthworks when a cannon was accidentally fired within the city and he was hit in the neck by the cannon ball.

Charles plaque, Carlisle

Charles rode into Carlisle on the 17th, accompanied by pipers. His made his quarters at Highmore House in English Street where he remained till the 21st. Highmore House is long gone, its site filled by the Marks and Spencer store in the town centre pedestrian precinct. It

bears an inscription on the front stating that it stands on the site of Highmore House, and at either corner there is another inscription, one stating that it was Charles's headquarters in

Cumberland plaque, Carlisle

1745, and the other more sinisterly that it was the headquarters of William, Duke of Cumberland in 1746. Many times when Charles and his army were in retreat and Cumberland's star was in the ascendancy, Cumberland occupied the quarters that Charles had recently vacated.

At Highmore, councils were held to discuss the plan of action for the immediate future of the campaign. Four ideas were brought forward. They could march towards Newcastle and confront the recalcitrant Wade. They could return to Scotland and go on the defensive. They could remain at Carlisle and await the rising of the English Jacobites, or they could continue the advance southwards towards London. The last option was agreed upon. Charles's spies had reported the readiness of the English people to rise and support the House of Stuart. Assurances of support from Jacobite sympathisers in England had been received. It was believed that an advance south would have the English rising to throw off the shackles of the Hanoverian regime.

CHAPTER 6

South to Derby

DURING THE MARCH SOUTH, the army was split into two roughly equal halves. The reason for this was that winter was now taking its icy grip, and when the first half of the army marched on from one town, the second half could commandeer the quarters vacated that morning by their compatriots, in the hope that enough billets would be found to save anyone from having to sleep in the open. Putting this arrangement into action, Lord George Murray left Carlisle with his troops on Wednesday 20 November, with Charles following on the 21st. A garrison of 150 men was left in charge of Carlisle.

The march south from Carlisle followed more or less exactly the route of the A6, which was built following the line of the ancient roads from centre of population to centre of population. The A6 has been superceded by the M6 motorway which follows a more direct route, but if you wish to take the original route of Charles's army, the A6 does the job.

The first night Lord George halted at Penrith, and the following day, the 21st, he marched his men on to Shap. When Charles arrived at Penrith, he lodged for the night in the George and Dragon Inn in the town centre. (MAP B18) Sometime before 1800 the George and Dragon was converted into a private dwelling, then around 1900 it became Prince Charlie's Restaurant. Today it is back in its original guise, being the George

George Hotel, Penrith

Hotel, looking not very different from how it was in Charles's day. It stands in Devonshire Street, near the clock which is a famous landmark in Penrith. The hotel's hanging sign is a portrait of Prince Charlie.

The weather took a turn for the worse, and ahead lay much higher ground which had snow and ice on the summits. Lord George Murray's soldiers had already made the crossing over the hills to Kendal, and on the 23rd Charles followed. Before doing the research for this book I had always driven south using the M6, but following the Jacobite army's route, I drove over the old Shap summit on the A6. The grandeur of the scenery does not detract from the terrain and distance that the Highlanders covered. One of the main things that struck me again and again while driving the routes was the huge distances that a fully laden army could cover in the course of a day, and in this case, short winter days, often in driving snow and sleet. An army can only move as fast as its slowest marchers, which makes some of the distances covered humbling indeed.

The highest point of the A6 between Penrith and Kendal has a lay-by with magnificent views and a cairn with a plaque which commemorates the locals who helped stranded drivers in winter in the early days of motoring. Looking out over the high tops and bleak moorland, you can imagine the tartan-clad clansmen wending their way south to help restore the direct descendent of the original Ard Righ, the High King of Scotland, to his rightful throne.

Reaching Kendal, Charles's residence for the night was Stricklandgate House which still stands in the town's Stricklandgate. (MAP C2) It is

Stricklandgate House, Penrith

now an art gallery and coffee shop with a plaque on its front wall testifying its Bonnie Prince Charlie connection, and 'Prince Charlie's House' in white lettering on the front door.

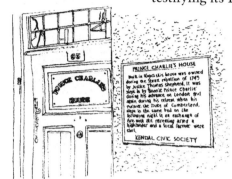

The following day, Sunday 24 November, Lord George Murray marched his section onward to Lancaster, Charles following on the 25th. (MAP C3) His quarters for the night were probably a building in Church Street which for many years

Stricklandgate plaque

has been the local Conservative Club. Some sources say that this was the actual building he stayed in, but it bears a little plaque on its front wall which states that Charles lodged near this site at a Mrs Livesay's house. While in Lancaster, the visitor should take a look at the castle, the core of this ancient city.

The following day the march continued, still following the line of the A6, towards Preston.

It is reported that Charles rarely mounted a horse on these long marches, preferring to march on foot, in kilt and plaid, bearing targe and claymore, to act as an inspiration to the loyal clansmen. In the chill of winter, the crossing of icy rivers would have been bracing to say the least. The clothing of the Gael was not designed for fickle fashion. The plaid was the perfect garb for the inhabitants of the mountainous north of Scotland. It would fan out and float while

Conservative Club, Lancaster

rivers were forded, and it would drip dry afterwards without chafing the legs. At night it would be taken off and its wearer would wrap himself up in its voluminous folds, so that it acted as a type of early sleeping bag. On the march in bad weather the excess top pleats could be opened out a little so that the upper half of the body was covered in a kind of shawl. Modern brogues (*brog* is the Gaelic for shoe) have a pattern of punched pieces of leather on their uppers. This is a nod to the fact that the light leather shoes of the Highlanders had holes punched through their uppers simply to allow water to flow out, as the land was very wet, especially in winter.

Conservative Club plaque

A still prevalent misconception is that each clan was identifiable by the tartan that they wore. Various Highlanders captured after Culloden posed for portraits, and most of them are wearing several different designs. Some have differing socks to plaid, plaid to waistcoat or coat, and coat to bonnet. Clan could generally tell friend from foe by the sprig of flower or plant worn in the bonnet. In the case of the Jacobite army, they wore the White Cockade symbolising the white rose of Scotland. Many Jacobite artefacts bear images of this little white rose, especially Jacobite wine glasses and the like. Many examples survive and are on display in various museums.

A grim shadow was beginning to form in the minds of the Jacobite leaders as they marched south through England. There had been no surge of support in England as they expected. Apart from a few individuals enlisting in the cause, they were met with what seemed to be a general indifference on the part of the English. The population of England was ten times that of Scotland, and the lack of support must have been a great worry.

Lord George arrived in Preston on the 25th, and as no invasion force from Scotland had ever reached further south than the River Ribble, he and his troops crossed the river and camped in the villages to the south so that no superstition on the part of the Highlanders could be brought to bear on the situation. A Jacobite army had previously reached as far as Preston in 1715. In the time of Robert the Bruce, fast-moving hobelars, or lightly-armed horsemen, had made raids as far south as Preston.

Lord George's division remained in the Preston area, so that when Charles came up the next day, the whole army was again gathered in the one place. (MAP C4)

While in Preston Charles had stayed at Mitre Court which stood at the entry to the Straight Shambles. The Guild Hall in Preston, seen on television as the venue for snooker championships, stands on the site of the Shambles (the market, from the word 'shamble', the name for a covered stall). Preston library and museum stands directly opposite the Guild Hall. In order to swell their war coffers, the Jacobites made demands for a sum of money to be raised by the magistrates of Preston. This money was delivered to the Jacobite officers at their headquarters in the White Bull Inn. This inn has survived and is today named the Old Bull. It stands in Church Street. Facing the Guild Hall and taking a turn to your right, the Old Bull is visible across the road when you reach the junction at the end of the street.

Old Bull Inn, Preston

An eye witness account of Charles's appearance in Preston has survived. 'He has marched from Carlisle on foot at the head of his army, he was dressed in a Scotch plaid, a blue silk waistcoat with silver lace,and a Scotch bonnet with J.R. on it.' The J.R. refers to his father, James Rex.

On 29 November the whole army marched the 14 miles to Wigan. (MAP C5) Charles made his headquarters at the Old Manor House which stood in the Bishopsgate. I made enquiries at the museum in Wigan to ascertain whether this building still survived and I was told that locally it was believed Charles lodged in a pub named the Tudor Inn which could be seen at the far side of the bus

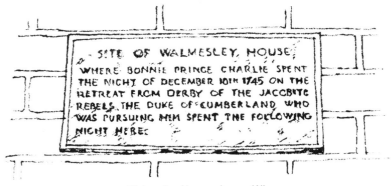

Walmesley House plaque, Wigan

station. I took a look at this building, and although it had been built in the Tudor Style, it seemed to be of a much later date of construction. I walked across the bus station to the site of the Bishopsgate which is marked on older maps of Wigan. There is a modern brick building named Walmesley House on the site of the Old Manor House and it has a plaque on the wall facing the bus station entrance announcing its Bonnie Prince Charlie connection. (It is always worth looking around at various options.)

Unknown to Charles, one of his sergeants named Dickson had walked to Manchester on the 28th and marched into the town centre with a drummer and a whore (many old accounts quaintly call her his mistress) and announced that the Highland army was close at hand and the town should show its support for the Stuart cause. Many inhabitants, scared that the Jacobites were so close, were afraid to confront Dickson, but as the day wore on the crowd grew bolder and made to lay hands on him. Dickson calmly put his blunderbuss to his shoulder, and circling, informed the crowd that he would blow out the brains of anyone who dared to put a finger upon him. A group of Manchester Jacobites, some 500 strong, appeared on the scene and strengthened Dickson's position, and he began to demand recruits for the army.

Charles, accompanied by his full force, did not appear in Manchester till the following day at about 2pm, and they were surprised to say the least to find the town in the hands of Dickson who had raised what became known as the Manchester Regiment. (MAP C6)

Charles took up quarters in the house of a Mr Dickenson in Market Street Lane. This building was later known as the Palace Inn but was demolished during the 1800s. It stood in the old town of Manchester, and, like the Shambles in Preston, is now a distant memory, nearly all the old buildings having been swept away in the name of progress.

A little reminder of these days exists to give us an idea of how things once were. Market Place and Market Street Lane and the rest of Manchester's shambles stood where the Arndale Shopping Centre is today. A couple of old buildings had survived, however, and these were physically lifted and moved before building work began. Sinclairs Oyster Bar, mentioned in records dating back to the 14th century, also stood in Market Place and was moved to its new site in 1971. The Old Wellington Pub, built in 1552 during the reign of Edward VI of England, stood in Market Place and was moved to its new site in 1974. They now stand in the thorough-fare called Cathedral Gates, between the Cathedral Church of St Mary, St Denys and St George and the Arndale Centre. Both were damaged by the blast of the IRA bomb in 1996, and repair work was completed in February 1997. They are an absolute delight and

Shambles, Manchester

are both open to the public, serving their original function. In these buildings we can see a little of the Manchester that the Jacobite army saw in 1745.

Detachments of troops were sent out from Manchester to Warrington and Altringham, making the Hanoverians think that a move would be made through Chester to Wales where it was believed Jacobite sympathies were very strong. But this was all a ploy, because on Sunday 1 December the march south was continued. Charles, with part of the army, forded the Mersey near Stockport. There had been a bridge here but it had been demolished to try to hinder his progress. The rest of his forces crossed the river at Cheadle and Gathey.

That night's halt was at Macclesfield where Charles spent the night at a house in

Charles's lodgings, Macclesfield

the Jordansgate in the town centre. (MAP C7) This building was later known as Cumberland House and is today the Cumberland Surgery, in use as a surgery and health centre. It has a little plaque on its wall announcing its status as a historic building, but its Jacobite association is not mentioned.

It was around this time that news was received that an army under William, Duke of Cumberland, was preparing to intercept

Greystones, Leek

and halt Charles's progress. Cumberland was at Lichfield, and it was decided to push on with all speed in the direction of Derby.

On Tuesday 3 December the entire army marched to Leek, following the route of the modern A528. (MAP C8)

Charles stayed in Leek with a handful of men and some reports state that he slept at a house in Market Place. Market Place is the old market square. Enquiring locally, I was told that Charles and his officers first knocked on the door of the vicarage which still stands in Stockwell Street, just opposite Market Place. The vicar's wife is said to have refused to answer the door, so a move was made further down Stockwell Street to a 17th-century building named Greystones. This picturesque building is today Greystones Tea Room. I was assured that this had been Charles's quarters.

Vicarage, Leek

While he remained in Leek, the army set off southwards towards Ashbourne around midnight. (MAP C9) The fact that they set off then is surprising. After all, it was December, and the countryside between Leek and Ashbourne is hilly enough to make a march in complete darkness quite eventful. There may have been a clear moonlit sky, of course, but if that was the case it would probably have been very frosty.

Ashbourne is a picturesque little town with some ancient houses near the church. Most impressive is the Grammar School which was founded in 1585 by Elizabeth 1 of England. The walls of this old building are completely covered in graffiti from ground level to head height – not graffiti in the modern sense, but names carved into the stonework of the walls, obviously done by generations of schoolchildren.

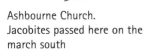

While the main body of the Highland army remained at Ashbourne, an advance guard followed the line of the A52 and on the 4th rode into Derby and demanded the town make arrangements for quartering the army. As the main body

Ashbourne Church. Jacobites passed here on the march south

marched on towards Derby, Charles left Leek and paused at Ashbourne, where he dined at an inn named The Three Horse Shoes which no longer exists. He then continued to Derby, arriving there on the evening of the 4th. (MAP C10) His quarters were in Exeter House, the mansion of Lord Exeter in Full Street. This mansion was demolished in 1854, but on its site in Full Street today is an impressive modern equestrian statue of Charles which stands on a stretch of parkland by the courts and police station.

A description of Charles's Highland infantry survives from this time – 'a parcel of shabby, pitiful-looking fellows mixed up with old men and boys: dressed in dirty shirts, without breeches, and wore their stockings made of plaid not much above halfway up their legs, and some without shoes, or next to none and numbers of them so fatigued with their long march that they really commanded our pity rather than our fear.' Many of these poor souls had marched all the way from Glenfinnan in winter weather. Driving their route of march, or even sections of it, makes you realise the vastness of this undertaking, and your respect can only soar for the individuals who covered these long miles on foot, bearing their weapons and belongings on their backs.

Charles Statue, Derby

The Highland army was now within 120 miles of London. Reaching Derby brought the Jacobites into England's soft underbelly. The rolling countryside of the north was left behind. Between Derby and London the landscape is much flatter, with the poplar-edged fields that Scots equate with the English south east. Topographically there was not much to stand in the way of determined soldiers.

Charles's spirits must have been soaring, knowing that a few days would see him in London. But a shock awaited him when he went into council with his commanders. 'Retreat,' they said. Charles was flabbergasted.

His officers pointed out that Cumberland was in charge of an army of some 12,000 men, based at Lichfield, only 25 miles south-west of Derby. Charles argued that they could easily out-pace them and head directly to London, but his officers reminded him that Wade's army was still somewhere to their rear, the same force that had been at Newcastle while they were at Carlisle. It was also believed that an army was gathering at Finchley on the north side of London to block their progress. Although this was only a myth, unfortunately the Jacobites believed it. It was even more unfortunate that they did not know the consternation that their presence was causing in London. The news that the Jacobites were at Derby reached London on Friday 6 December, and panic ensued. There was a run on the Bank of England. King George had all his valuables loaded onto yachts at Tower Quay with orders for them to be ready to sail at a moment's notice. London-based Jacobites made ready to welcome Charles with open arms. In London this day was remembered as Black Friday, but it was an even blacker day for the Highland army.

Charles's officers pointed out that there had been none of the expected manifestations of support since they had marched into England, and this was the final straw. The decision to retreat was taken. Charles is said to have remarked that he wished he was buried twenty feet underground.

Looking back and knowing that this retreat was to culminate in the slaughter of Culloden, one can only wish that the advance had gone ahead and wonder what the outcome of a march into London would have achieved. If Charles had ascended the throne, would he have been ousted within weeks, or would opposition have evaporated? Would we have had tartan and Gaelic at Westminster today?

Of all the sites I visited in England the one that affected me most was the bridge at Swarkstone, 6 miles south of Derby town

Swarkstone Bridge

centre on the A514. (MAP CII) The advance guard of Charles's army was sent to take this vital bridge over the River Trent. It was the nearest point to London reached by Jacobite soldiers. Swarkstone is an ancient structure. At its northern end is the large stone bridge carrying the road over the Trent. From this bridge a stone causeway, which still carries the modern road, runs south for over a mile to rising ground. I can only imagine that the river would have flooded the fields in time of spate, and the causeway was vital for communication with the countryside south of Derby. It puts me a little in mind of Stirling Bridge at the time of William Wallace, with its causeway running from the Forth north to the Abbey Craig, but I have never come across another structure like Swarkstone.

Once I had crossed the river and driven the causeway in both directions, I parked and walked along the riverbank a short distance and then over the surrounding fields. I could see in my mind's eye the detachment of Highlanders standing on the bridge, waiting for their fellows to appear and begin the march for Loughborough and London. But their fellows never appeared, and their orders to retreat would have come as a surprise. They must have wondered what on earth was taking place in their commanders' minds as they shouldered their weapons and headed back to Derby. Two hundred and fifty-four years after this event I stood on the bridge. I could feel London away to the south – unseen, but sensed. A few days' easy march away. Then I climbed aboard my own steed and turned it towards the north.

Edinburgh
Charles rides triumphantly down the Royal Mile.

Edinburgh

Edinburgh Castle
As it looked at the time of the '45.

Prestonnans

Prestonpans
Tranent church in the background. The A1 now crosses this view.

Carlisle Castle

CHAPTER 7

Retreat to the Border

THE HIGHLANDERS WERE GIVEN orders to pack up their equipment and march. It was only when they started to notice landmarks they had passed en route to Derby that they realised they were heading north. Consternation reigned. Their officers pointed out that the expected rising of the English Jacobites had not taken place. Retreat, they argued, and they could consolidate. The raising of troops for the cause was still taking place in Scotland. They could swell their ranks with the new recruits then march south again. Cumberland at Lichfield did not see it that way, however. He saw retreat as a sign of weakness, and as soon as word reached him that Charles and his army were heading north, he marched his men in pursuit.

William, Duke of Cumberland, had experience of warfare on the continent. He was a son of King George, and therefore through dynastic connections he and Charles could have named each other cousin. Propaganda plays its part in the writing of history, of course, which helps explain the phrase 'history is written by the winners'. Cumberland, who was a fat youth, is usually portrayed as a very English gentleman. However, German is said to have been his first language, not English, and he would give his orders in Latin, the one tongue that he and many of his officers had in common.

The Jacobites headed north, following exactly the route they had taken coming south. The first night's halt was at Ashbourne, Charles taking quarters in Ashbourne Hall, which stands to the east of the village. It is assumed that Charles stayed in the same premises in each town that he had occupied on the march south.

Many of the Highlanders hoped that Cumberland would actually speed his advance, as they were ready and eager to engage with his forces. It would seem that Charles himself hoped that this would happen, and over the course of the next few days he tried to slow up the pace of retreat in the hope that battle could be joined, but his officers hastened the army back towards Scotland. They camped at Leek on the 7th, Macclesfield on the 8th, and Manchester on the 9th.

To give some idea of the nature of Cumberland, he had captured a Jacobite straggler at Macclesfield. This individual was hung as a spy and his body was skinned and sold to a local doctor for 4s 6d (about 22p). The skin was given to a local tanner, but he found that human skin was not strong enough to make any of his usual items, and he eventually buried it.

On entering Manchester, the Highlanders were confronted by a baying mob of townsfolk, shouting derisively at the retreating army. In Wigan the next day, 10 December, an assassination attempt was made on Charles's life by a staunch Hanoverian, but his aim was poor and his shot went wide of the mark.

The 11th saw the Highlanders back in Preston where they halted for a day to give some rest to the hard-travelled army, then Lancaster was reached on the 13th. There Charles took enough of a stand to have the idea of a showdown with Cumberland taken seriously. A spot two miles south of Lancaster was decided on as the best place for battle to be joined, but in the event it did not happen and the retreat continued.

From Lancaster Charles sent a body of horsemen forward to Scotland, under the command of the Duke of Perth, to make contact with a party of reinforcements that were known to have gathered at Perth. When they reached Kendal they were attacked by a group of local militia. The story had been spread by the Hanoverians that Charles's army had been defeated in battle, and the stragglers were heading for Scotland with the victorious Cumberland in pursuit. This information had the effect of rousing the locals, keen to show they were on the side of the victors, and the Duke of Perth had to retire to warn Charles of the danger that awaited him.

The main army reached Kendal on the 15th, then marched on towards Penrith on the 17th. The rearguard of the Jacobite army was somewhat delayed negotiating the road over Shap summit, north of Kendal, and when they were having difficulties approaching Penrith, horsemen from the Hanoverian forces appeared on the hilltops to the south. In view of this threat, the Jacobites halted for the evening, with the option of making a stand if need be in the little village of Clifton, a mile or two south of Penrith. (MAP CI) Clifton stands to your left as you drive south on the M6, just after junction 40.

Four divisions of Highlanders were involved on this occasion. They were Glengarry's Regiment, Roy Stewart's Regiment, the Stewarts of Appin, and Cluny MacPherson's Regiment. They were dispersed around the village, their northernmost point close to the River Lowther, then they spread out south-west and south-east round the old church and into the fields to create a defensive circle around the northern half of the village. They had no idea of the strength of the forces arrayed against them. Night fell, and in

Clifton Church

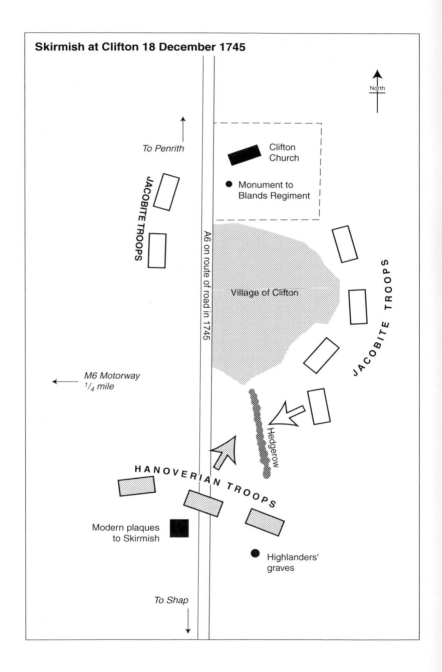

Skirmish at Clifton 18 December 1745

North

To Penrith

JACOBITE TROOPS

Clifton Church

Monument to Blands Regiment

A6 on route of road in 1745

Village of Clifton

JACOBITE TROOPS

M6 Motorway
1/4 mile

Hedgerow

HANOVERIAN TROOPS

Modern plaques to Skirmish

Highlanders' graves

To Shap

those pre-street lighting days on a December night the darkness must have been ominously impenetrable.

Hanoverian troops spread out and started to deploy on the other side of the hedges round the fields where the Highlanders lay. These hedges would not have been tight clipped like they are today, but would be very wide, unkempt and rambling, probably with holes and gaps that a man could push through. The fact that the Hanoverians were on the move soon came to the Highlanders' attention. Cluny MacPherson's Regiment was ordered to push through the hedge in front of it and advance to the next one. One of the Highlanders reported, 'Through the hedge we made our way with the help of our dirks, the pricks being very uneasy, I assure you, to our loose tailed lads.' As they approached the second hedge, the Hanoverians let fly with a full volley from their muskets. Luckily the darkness prevented too much injury on the side of the Highlanders, only a few falling with bullet wounds. Lord George Murray immediately drew his sword, shouting, 'Claymore!'. With a shriek of steel the Highlanders drew theirs and ran, smashing their way through the hedge and slashing at everyone in their path.

The Redcoats, members of General Bland's Regiment, broke and fled, running to try and cross a ditch to their rear. When the Highlanders reached the ditch, Cluny MacPherson stopped his men from further pursuit, darkness preventing any real knowledge of what lay before them. He halted all except one. Angus of Knappach was an extremely powerful individual and an accomplished swordsman, but he was deaf and did not hear the command to halt. He ran after the fleeing Redcoats, slashing with his sword, and it was only when he had far outdistanced his fellow clansmen that he realised his was a solo effort. He turned and shouted back, 'Why do you stop – I can see plenty more further on!'. When he eventually got back to his own lines he announced his displeasure at having to return when there were so many more

Redcoats to kill. It is individual acts of bravery such as this that make history come alive for me, and let us catch a glimpse of the calibre of the men in those days.

This brief battle became known as the Skirmish at Clifton, and

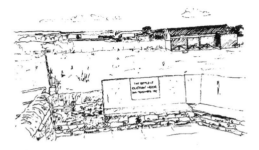

it was the last battle to be fought on English soil.

Lord George Murray successfully withdrew his men from the village a mile or two north to Penrith. Cumberland sent a report to London

Clifton plaque (1)

saying that he had managed to clear the 'rebels' from Clifton. This does not seem to have been the case, as the Hanoverians were repelled, and the Jacobites retired when they were good and ready.

By the time the rearguard reached Penrith, the main body of

the army had marched on towards Carlisle. The rearguard followed. They marched from Kendal to Carlisle, a distance of 36 miles, had gone almost three days without sleep, had fought at Clifton on the way, and had lost none of the artillery that had been entrusted to their charge.

Several mementoes of the fight at Clifton still stand. The small church at the north end of the village remains as it was in

Clifton plaque (2)

1745. As you enter the grave-yard, on your right stands a modern gravestone to the memory of the troops of Bland's Regiment who fell that day. Eleven were slain and another 30 were badly wounded. Travelling half a mile or so south through the straggling village, you come across a little walled inshot projecting into a field on your right. There is a well here and a memorial tablet to the fight. There is another small plaque facing towards a tree planted on the 250th anniversary of the Skirmish.

Bland's Memorial,
Clifton Churchyard

Most poignant of all, however, are the graves of the five Highlanders of Cluny's Regiment who died in the burst of musket fire. A little south of the plaques, on the left side of the road, is a farm with various out-buildings. A track leads down the north side of the buildings, and under an old gnarled tree just past the buildings is an old grave-stone. Here the Highlanders lie, far from the heather-covered mountains of home. On my last visit, a few roses, the little white roses of Scotland, lay dry and blackened around the gravestone, put there by some previous visitor.

I first heard of the Skirmish at Clifton just prior to beginning this book, so the discovery of the graves was a welcome surprise. I have driven south along the M6 a great many times, ignorant of the fact that some fellow Scots lay so close to the road's edge. From the grave you can hear the rumble of heavy trucks carrying their goods to far destinations.

On arrival at Carlisle, Charles was presented with letters, one of which was from the French king, promising aid and asking Charles not to risk his men in any sort of decisive battle till he was fortified by French troops. Another letter came from Lord Strathallan who had been gathering reinforcements at Perth. He stated that a fine army was mustered and ready to take part in the Prince's cause. In light of all this, it was decided to leave a holding force at Carlisle while the rest of the army moved north. Charles was sure that in a week or two he would be marching south again for London, well reinforced and equipped.

Four hundred men remained at Carlisle. They comprised the Manchester Regiment who, not surprisingly, did not want to leave England, the wounded from Clifton and a few men from the Highland regiments. On the 20th the main body of the army marched for the border.

Highlanders' graves, Clifton

Cumberland and his forces wasted no time and appeared before the walls of Carlisle on the 21st. Cannon were deployed, and a heavy barrage rained down upon the castle and walls. The Jacobite garrison managed to hold out until 30 December when they flew the white flag of surrender above the city. In the light of Charles's magnanimous treatment of the garrison of Carlisle when it was captured on his march south, the Jacobites must have thought that they would be treated with an equal courtesy, but they were to discover the bestial nature of Cumberland. At 4 o'clock in the afternoon the gates were opened and the Hanoverians marched into the town. The Jacobite officers were imprisoned in the castle, while the rank and file were confined within the cathedral.

Both Carlisle Castle and Cathedral are open to the public. The great central keep of the castle dates from 1092. Both Wallace and Bruce beseiged the castle, Mary Queen of Scots was held captive there for a time, and Edward I held a parliament there, so it is a place steeped in history. The cathedral was built between 1092 and 1419 and some of the stained glass is original 14th century. The castle contains exhibitions of Carlisle at the time of the

Jacobite occupation, as does the city's Tullie House Museum which also has audio-visuals depicting the times of the Border Reivers, as well as a huge collection of Roman artefacts. (Hadrian's Wall runs close to the modern city.)

If they had only known the fate about to befall them, the Jacobites who were now prisoners would have been happy to fight to the last man for Carlisle. They were kept caged in various locations under extreme conditions until the following summer of 1746, when they were dragged to the English Gate of Carlisle and hung, before being cut down alive and suffering disembowelment – the English punishment for high treason. It is a dreadful end for any man to suffer, but it was especially so for these men who had marched the long road south from Glenfinnan, in foul winter weather, fighting for the rightful heir to the throne of both Scotland and England. But the Hanoverians had had a fright, and victors tend to be at their most vengeful when victory has been snatched from the jaws of defeat.

It is reported that one Highlander was visited by his sweetheart before his execution, and it was their tearful parting that inspired the words to the famous song,

> Oh you'll take the high road
> And I'll take the low road
> And I'll be in Scotland afore ye
> For me and my true love
> Will never meet again
> On the bonnie bonnie banks of Loch Lomond.

The meaning, of course, was that the condemned man's spirit would immediately fly home. I can understand that. I wouldn't want to spend eternity anywhere else but Scotland.

CHAPTER 8

Back into Scotland

CHARLES AND HIS ARMY crossed the River Esk between Gretna and Longtown on 20 December, Charles's birthday, and once more stood upon Scottish soil. The Esk was in spate, and the men had crossed in one huge body – 2,000 were in the water at one time according to Lord George Murray. One report claimed that some young women, determined to follow their highland lovers, were washed away by the strength of the current. Charles is said to have been fording the river on his horse when one unfortunate soldier lost his footing. Charles managed to grab the man's long hair and hold him until his fellows came to his aid.

Once across, fires were lit and the pipers began to play, the Highlanders dancing to shake off the chill of the winter river. This event is commemmorated in the stirring song 'Wi' a hundred pipers an a' an a' '.

The army split into two columns of march. One arm, commanded by Lord George Murray, would take the route of the modern M74 northwards, passing through Ecclefechan and Lockerbie towards Moffat. The other would proceed through Annan to Dumfries, then follow the course of the River Nith to Drumlanrig. This column was led by Charles.

A cottage and B&B establishment in the village of Gretna bears the name Prince Charlie's Cottage, although Charles actually spent the night of the 20th in the town of Annan. (MAP B19) There must be many houses where Charles stopped to eat or drink, and local traditions connecting him with various premises may have some grounding in fact. The Buck Inn in Annan, Charlie's quarters, stands on the north side of the main thoroughfare. Though some-

Annan. Charles stayed in building second from left.

what altered it is still a licenced premises, now named the Auberge. It has a sundial and two carved heads on its frontage, the heads supposedly likenesses of Charles. It also carries the dates 1700-1903, the date of the original construction and the date of the building of the new facade.

Leaving Annan at 10 o'clock the following morning, the 21st, the column followed the line of the A75 to Dumfries, where Charles

Next shop, Dumfries

took up quarters in a mansion on the west side of High Street. (MAP B20) This building later became the Commercial Hotel, and today it is the Next store, painted neatly in black and white. At first floor level, some of the original fittings of the house can still be seen, such as fireplaces and even old oil paintings, hidden behind the racks of clothing in the menswear department!

Charles remained at Dumfries until Monday 23 December, many of the Highlanders passing the time by relieving the citizens of Dumfries of their footwear, their attitude being that the army's need was greater than that of the populace.

They marched north, following the valley of the River Nith, and that night, the 23rd, the men were divided between the village

Drumlanrig Castle

of Thornhill and Drumlanrig Castle. Charles slept at Drumlanrig. (MAP B21) Originally constructed by the Douglas family, the owner in 1745 was the Duke of Queensberry. Whilst there, the Highlanders slaughtered some 40 sheep for their supper, and threw 'some sort of liquid' over the portrait of William III. This portrait today hangs in the staircase hall of the building, the damage still evident. The room where Charles slept can be visited, and several artefacts of his stay are displayed within the house.

On the 24th the march continued up Nithsdale, some of the men billeting in Sanquhar, the rest striking north-east into the Lowther Hills and resting at Wanlockhead and Leadhills. Charles stayed at the ancient and historic Douglas Castle, just east of the Lanarkshire village of the same name. (MAP B22) Douglas became famous through the devotion of James Douglas to King Robert the Bruce – it was he who carried Bruce's heart on crusade. All that remains of the castle today is one incomplete tower which stands forlorn on a spur of raised ground above the Douglas Water. In 1745 a sword, gifted to Douglas by Bruce on his deathbed in 1329, was on display within the castle. This sword was carried on crusade by Douglas, and after his death it was returned to Scotland, accompanying his remains which were interred within St Bride's church in Douglas village. The sword bears a later inscription announcing its Bruce connection. Not to let a useful weapon go to waste, one of the Highlanders took the sword and it was used at the battles of Falkirk and Culloden before being returned to the Douglas family. It is now kept at the Hirsel, the seat of the Home family just outside Coldstream, but is not currently on public display.

Next day, Christmas Day 1745, the march continued to Hamilton where Charles took up quarters within the now demolished Hamilton Palace. (MAP B23) This was a massive stately pile which stood on the flatland between the town of Hamilton and the Clyde. All that remains of it today are a few outbuildings, in use as the town's museum. The Mausoleum, a huge domed structure surrounded by trees beside the M74, was the last resting place of generations of Hamiltons and boasts one of the most impressive echoes to be heard in these islands.

The following morning Charles enjoyed some hunting on the parks belonging to the Duke of Hamilton at Châtelherault. This building has been restored to its former glory and is open to the public. It stands a mile or two from Hamilton, and access is gained from the Hamilton to Larkhall road. The landscape surrounding Châtelherault is awe-inspiring, the gorge of the River Avon, the ruins of Cadzow Castle, and the forest of oaks planted by David I being just some of the attractions.

That afternoon Charles proceeded to Glasgow via Bothwell

Bridge. (MAP B24) Lord George Murray had already reached Glasgow with his section of the army which had marched by the more easterly route, basically following the line of the A74 northwards, and had arrived the previous day, Christmas Day. Charles stayed in Shawfield House which is long gone but stood at what is now the junction of Argyle Street and Glassford Street, adjacent to the Marks and Spencer store. The house had large gardens and orchards which would have stretched back to Ingram Street, where the Italian Centre is now. It was at Shawfield House that Charles first met 20-year-old Clementina Walkinshaw, a young lady of good stock, who was later to become his mistress.

Glasgow was not too enamoured of Jacobitism, and much animosity was displayed towards Charles's forces, so much so, indeed, that it seems most of the Highland chiefs were of a mind to sack and burn the entire city. Cameron of Locheil took great exception to this suggestion, and threatened to withdraw his clansmen and return home. In light of this the threat was not carried out, and ever since, whenever the current Cameron of Locheil has visited Glasgow, the city bells have rung out a carillon of welcome. Glasgow may have escaped the threat of burning, but the city was coerced into supplying the army with, among other things, 12,000 shirts, 6,000 coats and 6,000 pairs of hose.

On 2 January 1746 Charles decided to review his entire forces at an event held on Glasgow Green. He rode out to that part of Glasgow Green known as Fleshers Haugh, which stands over by Bridgeton, and much comment was made on the gallant and charming picture Charles presented. It is said that as he left Glasgow Green to return to Shawfield House via the Saltmarket, an attempt was made on his life. An individual drew a pistol, but it misfired.

The following day the army was again split into two columns of march, Lord George Murray taking one along the route of the modern A80, halting for the night at Cumbernauld. Charles followed the route of the A803 through Kirkintilloch, halting for the night at Kilsyth.

On the 4th the march continued through Bonnybridge and Denny. Charles stayed that night at Bannockburn House. The next day a drummer was sent to the gates of Stirling to demand the town's surrender, but the garrison shot at him and he had to flee, leaving his drum behind. Various negotiations took place over the next few days, and the magistrates of Stirling, realising their position was untenable, eventually opened up the town to the Jacobite forces on Wednesday 8 January. But the castle was still in the hands of the Hanoverian forces.

Over the few days while Charles was at Bannockburn House, many new recruits joined his forces, many from Perth where mustering had been taking place. Meanwhile, a Hanoverian army was mustering in Edinburgh under the command of General Hawley who had something like 8,000 troops at his disposal. Hawley was an arrogant man, and bragged to his fellow officers of the easy victory he would achieve against Charles's highland rabble.

The Jacobites decided to try to take Stirling Castle. Earthworks were created to give foundations and cover for a row of cannon to batter the castle into submission. These earthworks were begun in the old graveyard of the Church of the Holy Rood, just behind the townhouse known as Mar's Wark. The people of Stirling became alarmed, realising that exchange of cannon shot would undoubtedly cause great damage to the town, and a deputation approached Charles to beseech him to reconsider. Charles acceded to their demands and new entrenchments were built on the hill to the north of the castle.

Word reached the Jacobites that General Hawley had begun to move westwards from Edinburgh to come to the relief of Stirling. On 16 January Hawley took up quarters at Callendar House in Falkirk, accompanied by his aide-de-camp, Captain Wolfe. This was the same Wolfe who was to go down in history as the general who fell at Quebec in 1759. Leaving 1,200 men to continue the siege at Stirling, Charles confidently marched his men to Plean Moor, expecting the Hanoverian army to advance to meet them.

CHAPTER 9

Falkirk

PLEAN MOOR STANDS NEAR the village of the same name, south-east of Stirling and Bannockburn. Facing Falkirk, it is bounded by the ever-widening Forth on the left and the edges of the Torwood on the right. The Jacobite army arrived on the moor on 15 January. That day and the next were uneventful, and the Highlanders were soon fretting at the inaction. That night, however, they could see the enemy camp fires in the distance, where they had camped between the old church at Falkirk and the low ground to the west (where the course of the Forth and Clyde canal would be cut a few years later). The lack of action proved so galling to the Highlanders, standing and waiting in battle order, that they informed their officers that if the enemy did not come soon, they would advance and engage them using their own initiative, even without a commander to lead them.

The following day, the 17th, Lord George Murray suggested that as the enemy was not coming to meet them, they should go and meet the enemy, the view being that if they used a little subterfuge, they might be able to reach the high ground behind Falkirk before the Hanoverians knew what they were doing and could take advantage of it. The Highland troops set off, turning south-west through the Torwood towards the River Carron at Dunipace, the intervening high ground hiding them from Hanoverian eyes at Falkirk. They came down to the bank of the Carron at Dunipace House, the home of Sir Archibald Primrose, one of Charles's most steadfast supporters. Dunipace House has long gone, bar one little fragment of tower containing a doocot which stands just east of the M876 beside the Hills of Dunipace cemetery. (MAP B25) Legend has it that it was at the old church at Hills of Dunipace that Wallace was raised by his uncle, the priest there, who taught him to value freedom above all things. The Jacobite army forded the Carron at the place known as Dunipace Steps. They swiftly crossed the level tract of land on the other side and reached the grassy ditches and mounds that remain of the Roman Antonine Wall, and sprinted for the hill behind Falkirk.

Callendar House, Falkirk

Hanoverian troops, having spotted the Highlanders disappearing into the dark recesses of the Torwood, communicated this information to General Hawley at Callendar House. Hawley reconnoitred from a nearby hill but declared there was nothing to worry about and returned to Callendar. Later in the day when his officers again informed him of their concerns regarding the Jacobites, Hawley reassured them that at the slightest movement on the part of their own troops the Highlanders would flee as fast as their legs would carry them. When word finally arrived that the Jacobites were well across the Carron and were racing to take the summit of the hill at South Bantaskine behind Falkirk, he seemed astonished. He found it hard to believe that not only were they not retreating but were actually on the offensive.

Forced to leave his early afternoon meal, he rode out to his troops, barking orders, his hair streaming in the wind – in the sudden panic he had not had time to don his headgear. He sent his

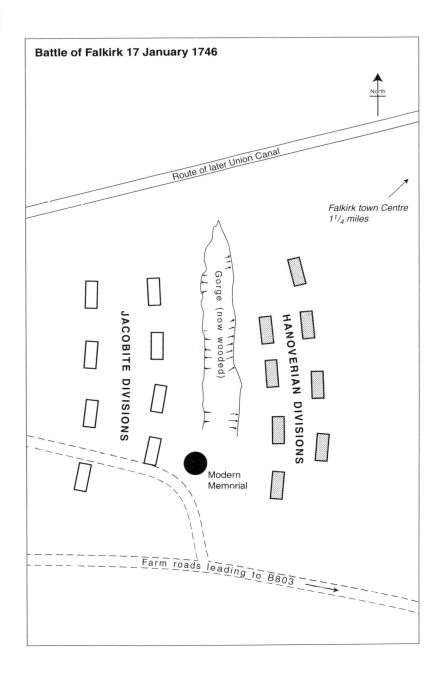

Battle of Falkirk 17 January 1746

North

Route of later Union Canal

Falkirk town Centre
1¹/₄ miles

Gorge (now wooded)

JACOBITE DIVISIONS

HANOVERIAN DIVISIONS

Modern
Memorial

Farm roads leading to B803

dragoons to try to gain the hill's summit before the Highlanders. A strong wind was blowing, and as the Hanoverians moved forward, it began to rain very heavily, the wind carrying the rain into the faces of the dragoons.

The Highlanders won the race to the hilltop and drew up their divisions in two lines, with a reserve to the rear. A natural ravine runs down the face of the hill, deepening the lower it goes, and the Highlanders formed up behind this, as if their front were defended by a large ditch. The Hanoverians drew up on the other side of the ravine, so the two armies were now facing each other only some 100 metres apart. The dragoons at the top of the ravine began to advance towards the Highlanders, mostly MacDonalds, who stood directly opposite. Shots were exchanged, then the MacDonalds drew their claymores and although their officers tried to restrain them, they charged across the top of the ravine, throwing themselves at the dragoons. The dragoons watched the onrushing line of tartan-clad figures, and as one body they broke and fled downhill, panicking the other Hanoverian troops.

A division of Hanoverian cavalry galloped downhill on their side of the ravine, offering an easy target for a barrage of rifle fire from the Highland divisions, and many fell. The MacDonalds ran slashing among the cavalry. A dead horse fell on MacDonald of Clanranald and he could not extricate himself. A fight to the death between a Highlander and a dragoon took place beside him, and fortunately for Clanranald, the Highlander managed to dispatch his enemy and then help to raise the weight of the dead beast and release his comrade.

Downhill, however, the situation was completely different. The Hanoverian ranks surged forward, crossing the ravine towards the Highland lines. The Highlanders immediately fired their muskets, then drew their swords and charged through the heavy rain, but the Hanoverian lines did not break. The Jacobite officers realised that they could easily be outflanked and shouted the order to halt. A sort of stalemate ensued. By this time it was after four in the afternoon and the light was beginning to go, the heavy January weather only adding to the gloom. Unaware of what had transpired at the top of the ravine, the Highlanders below had no idea if the day had been lost or won. Perhaps the Hanoverians had drawn back and regrouped in the darkness? The gloom probably saved the Hanoverians from defeat. It hid the fact that they had made a hasty withdrawal. The Highlanders would have doubled their efforts if they had realised their enemy was displaying any sort of weakness. It was only when Lord Kilmarnock, one of the Jacobite officers, reconnoitered forward to Callendar House and saw all the Hanoverian forces in utter confusion, hurrying along the main road eastwards in the direction of Edinburgh, that word was conveyed back to Charles and his officers – they had secured a complete victory. The Hanoverian forces had not only left the field but had abandoned Falkirk itself.

It was only later that details could be gathered with any accuracy: the Jacobites had lost perhaps 40 men, but over 100 were wounded. In comparison, the Hanoverians had some 400 killed. The greatest loss on the Jacobite side was the capture of MacDonald of Tirnadris, the hero of the opening action of the '45 at Highbridge in Lochaber. (MAP A10) He had fought with distinction through the whole campaign. After the rout of the Hanoverian forces at the top of the hill, he had approached a static body of men and exhorted them to join in the chase. He realised too late that due to the bad weather he had erroneously approached the enemy, who managed to take him captive. When the retreat was made, he was carried to Edinburgh then later transferred to Carlisle. He was described as 'a brave, undaunted, honest man, of a good countenance, and of a strong robust make'. He was to suffer the hideous death for treason at Carlisle on 18 October 1746.

Some of the Hanoverian prisoners were kept at Doune Castle.

They were allowed to exercise by walking on the high ramparts of the curtain walling. Seizing the moment, they used bedclothes tied together to make a makeshift rope, and six of them made their escape and got clean away.

There were two notable deaths on the Hanoverian side at Falkirk. Sir Robert Munro, chief of that clan, had led the Black Watch at the Battle of Fontenoy and was colonel of a regiment at Falkirk. He was admired by Hanoverians and Jacobites alike. As his men fled, he refused to move, and was attacked by six men of Locheil's regiment, Camerons and MacGregors. Munro killed two of his assailants, but another man, Calum na Ciabhaig (Malcolm of the ringlet) fired a pistol and struck Munro in the groin. He then jumped forward and caught Munro with two sword slashes, one of which was across the eyes, the other across the mouth. Munro died instantly. On seeing this, his brother Duncan ran forward to his sibling's aid, but was struck with a bullet in the chest then dispatched with a sword stroke. The two bodies were discovered the following day, stripped and lying in a pool. On hearing this, Charles ordered that they should have a decent burial. Although they had fought for the opposing side, the Highlanders respected the Munro brothers who came from Highland stock, and almost all the Jacobite officers attended their burial in the old churchyard at Falkirk. They were buried beside each other and a superb

Tomb at Falkirk

Tomb at Falkirk

monument was erected over them, inscribed with the circumstances of their death, one side written in Latin, the other in English. On my last visit, the monument had been badly defaced with spray paint.

Alongside the tomb of the Munros stands the memorial to William Edmondstoune of Cambus-Wallace. He was a captain-lieutenant in the Hanoverian forces, and his tomb was raised by the Dollar family, natives of Falkirk who had emigrated to the United States. The last resting place of two of Wallace's commanders, plus a celtic cross erected to the memory of the men of Bute who fought with Wallace at Falkirk in 1298, also stand in this churchyard.

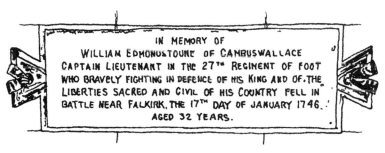

IN MEMORY OF
WILLIAM EDMONDSTOUNE OF CAMBUSWALLACE
CAPTAIN LIEUTENANT IN THE 27TH REGIMENT OF FOOT
WHO BRAVELY FIGHTING IN DEFENCE OF HIS KING AND OF THE
LIBERTIES SACRED AND CIVIL OF HIS COUNTRY FELL IN
BATTLE NEAR FALKIRK, THE 17TH DAY OF JANUARY 1746.
AGED 32 YEARS.

Plaque on grave at Falkirk Graveyard

The battlefield of Falkirk has changed very little over the years, and it is still possible to walk the ground and picture it as it was on 17 January 1746. The site is about a mile and a quarter south-west of Falkirk town centre, a little north of the B803 which runs from Falkirk High railway station towards Slamannan. A pointed-topped pillar monument commemorating the battle (marked on Ordnance Survey maps) stands just west of the top of the ravine alongside a narrow unclassified road. Parking at the monument is difficult, so it is better to turn left at the junction at the top of the hill and park somewhere along this slightly wider road. The ravine that separated the two armies is today covered with trees – presumably it was clear of heavy growth at the time of the battle. There are plans to construct a giant wheel to join the Forth and Clyde and Union canals several hundred metres north of the monument, so this may help in locating the site. Work began on the construction of the Forth and Clyde canal in 1768, only 22 years after the battle, which brings home the fact that the industrial revolution was already beginning at a time when claymores were still being wielded in Scotland's central belt.

Falkirk Churchyard

I recall visiting Falkirk as a teenager and enquiring about the location of Wallace's Battle of Falkirk. (MAP B26) At the information centre I was directed to the site of the Jacobite battle. Nearly everyone I asked looked completely nonplussed at the mention of Wallace's fight at Falkirk. The situation has gone full circle, as Wallace has risen again in the nation's psyche. The fact that Wallace fought here will probably be far more widely known now than that there was a later battle fought by the Highlanders under Bonnie Prince Charlie, due to phenomena like the motion picture *Braveheart*. But the clansmen had again prevailed against well-equipped, seasoned troops. General Hawley had had his balloon pricked, to say the least!

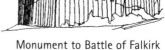

Monument to Battle of Falkirk

He sent a letter to the Duke of Cumberland stating that his heart was broken, that he had never seen such scandalous cowardice, that the second line of foot had run away without firing a shot.

After the battle, the Jacobite army entered Falkirk around 7pm. Between the battlefield and Falkirk itself stood a large mansion named Bantaskine, and the Hanoverian army had marched around the walls of this property in their race to try to reach the hilltop before the Highlanders. Bantaskine House is long gone, but there are a couple of mementoes preserved in the modern Howgate Shopping Centre in Falkirk. The main thoroughfare of this covered centre was originally the Bantaskine Port, leading out of town towards the house. It is hard to imagine today, watching people wandering around the shops, that this was the route that the rain-drenched Highland army marched into Falkirk High Street after their victory.

Three stained glass windows from Bantaskine House survived, and are mounted beside the escalators within the shopping centre. One is of Charles, one is of Lord George Murray, and the third is of John Drummond, another of Charles's commanders (MAP B27). The figures are about life size and are surmounted by coats of arms. A sign board before them tells their story. If you exit the Howgate Centre into the High Street and turn left, it is only a few yards to an opening on the right into Falkirk churchyard and its tombs.

Charles spent the night of the 17th in the home of a Mrs Graham, a staunch Jacobite. The site of this house in the High Street is now occupied by Dixons, the electrical retailer. It stands directly opposite the town steeple which today contains the Information Centre.

On the morning of the 18th a party of country people were gathered and employed to bury the dead from the battle. It was reported that as they neared the hillside, the stripped bodies looked like a flock of white sheep. It was only as they drew closer that they could see the terrible effects of the dirk and claymore in the gashes and mutilation apparent on the dead. A pit was dug on the battlefield and the bodies were unceremoniously thrown in.

One unfortunate incident took place in Falkirk after the battle. A Highlander had appropriated an English musket he had found on the battlefield. He did not realise it contained a double charge and he extracted just one of the balls, sticking the barrel out of the window to fire and clear the charge. Sadly, the remaining ball killed the young Colonel of the Glengarry regiment, Angus Og (Young Angus) MacDonald. The man was taken out of town by the outraged Glengarry men and shot. One report claimed that Charles ordered Angus's body to be interred in the tomb of Sir John de Graham, one of Wallace's commanders, in Falkirk churchyard, which seems a bit strange. Certainly, when Graham's tomb was opened in 1850, according to *An Account of the Principal Memorials in Falkirk Churchyard* by J. Reddoch McLuckie, only one body was discovered, about five feet down, lying on a gravel bed.

Although the Jacobites had marched several hundred miles from Glenfinnan to Derby and back to Falkirk, they had still never been defeated. They had won two major battles and every skirmish, including major incidents like Clifton. It seems extraordinary in the circumstances that they should be retreating further and further from London, their original destination.

Cumberland
Known throughout the Highlands as 'The Butcher' and characterised as such here.

Execution of Jacobite prisoners
This print of Carlisle Castle shows the aftermath of Cumberland's retaking of the city.

Culloden

This print of the aftermath of the battle dates from about 1840.

Inverness

Loch nan Uamh

Old print showing Charles's departure. A cairn marks the spot today.

Flora MacDonald
The Jacobite heroine is buried on the Isle of Skye.

CHAPTER 10

Further North

AFTER FALKIRK, CHARLES RETURNED to Bannockburn House where one of the guests was Clementina Walkinshaw whom he had first met in Glasgow. It is believed that an affair began between them.

The siege of Stirling Castle was recommenced with fresh vigour after the victory. Cannon were mounted on Lady's Hill and Gowan Hill, but a brief exchange of fire proved the castle garrison had the upper hand, as the Jacobite cannon were all dismounted from their positions by enemy fire, resulting in many casualties.

There was a great number of desertions after Falkirk. The edge of the Highlands was visible in the distance up by the head streams of the Forth. The sight of Ben Vorlich, Ben Lomond, Stuc a Chroin and Stobinian must have had many of the clansmen hankering after the sight of their own heather-covered slopes after their long march into the heartland of England, and many slipped away during the long winter nights.

Charles had truly expected a resurgence of appetite for another march south to England after the victory at Falkirk, but word came of Cumberland's arrival in Edinburgh with fresh regiments of troops. The chiefs decided to march back into the Highlands, and a communication to this effect was delivered to Charles at Bannockburn House. He was thunderstruck when he read the message. 'Good God!', he exclaimed, 'Have I lived to see this?' and he struck his head violently against the wall of his room. He began to suspect Lord George Murray of having an interest in thwarting his cause. Lord George had fought valiantly, but there seemed to be a clash of personalities, and perhaps an aloofness about Lord George that aroused Charles's suspicions. It was the first hint of a rift between them.

Charles penned a reply, part of which ran as follows: 'Is it possible that a victory and a defeat should produce the same effects, and that the conquerors should fly from an engagement, while the conquered are seeking it? Should we make the retreat you propose, how much more will that raise the spirits of our enemies and sink those of our own people? Can we imagine, that where we go the enemy will not follow, and at last oblige us to a battle which we now decline? Can we hope to defend ourselves at Perth, or keep our men together there, better than we do here? We must therefore continue our flight to the mountains, and soon find ourselves in a worse condition that we were in at Glenfinnan.'

Charles's eloquence, at least, is apparent in these lines. What he was predicting, unfortunately, was to come true. How much better it would have been to have had the daring to attack Cumberland where they stood, even perhaps at nearby Bannockburn of blessed memory, where the ancestors of Charles and his men had thwarted the ambitions of England.

On the evening of the last day of January 1746 the arrangements for the withdrawal were hammered out. Much time had been spent trying to force the garrison of Stirling Castle to capitulate, and this was obviously a major mistake. The Jacobite forces would have been better using their energies elsewhere. Even if Stirling had been taken and garrisoned, it might only have resulted in another 'Carlisle' once the Hanoverian forces approached. Charles spent the last night in the area at Bannockburn House, while Lord George Murray quartered at Easter Green Yards, a farm which is still there and stands about a mile north-east of Bannockburn House.

As the army prepared to march, Charles gave orders that any gunpowder or munitions that could not be removed from the temporary arsenal in St Ninian's church were to be destroyed. As these orders were carried out and barrels were taken to the rear of the church for disposal, one of the sentries noticed several villagers helping themselves to some of the stores. In order to frighten off the looters, the sentry discharged his musket in their general direction. Some of the sparks fell upon spilt powder which led towards the church door, and in an instant there was a massive explosion and the church disintegrated. One account states that 'barely an atom of the ancient church remained'. Many nearby houses were damaged by the blast, fourteen or fifteen people were killed, and many more were injured by flying debris.

Luckily the steeple of St Ninian's stood a little way from the church itself and survived intact – as it does to this day in the village of St Ninians a little to the south of Stirling. It is near the main route which approaches Stirling from the motorway junction south of the town, and many visitors must drive by it, oblivious to its history. St Ninian lived in the late 4th and early 5th centuries, so there may have been a church on this site from the earliest times although it is first mentioned in documents from the time of King David I.

A new church was built, but within the old churchyard there are some small remains of the one destroyed in the explosion. The rumour was spread by the Hanoverians that the church had been deliberately destroyed, but this was obviously false.

Cumberland, meanwhile, had advanced his men from Edinburgh to Linlithgow which he reached on 31 January. He took up quarters with many of his men within the venerable Linlithgow Palace, standing on the hill above Linlithgow Loch. Linlithgow Palace was the home of the Stewart Kings of

St Ninians

Scotland and was the birthplace of Mary Queen of Scots. It would have been crammed with artefacts from every era of Scottish history, not to mention tapestries and gifts from foreign lands. But alas, the building was set on fire on the morning of 1 February – whether by accident or design has never been established – but as Cumberland marched his men away, no attempt was made to extinguish the flames and the whole building burned, only the outer walls remaining. All the treasures were destroyed, even everyday items that would have been of immense interest today. But Bonnie Prince Charlie was a Stewart, and the House of Hanover would have needed no other reason to let the palace burn. Not only was the palace destroyed, but Cumberland made no mention of it in his communications, and no finger was ever pointed at a guilty party regarding a possible act of carelessness.

The palace is a vast structure, built around a central quadrangle. The ruins are open to the public, and you can only try to imagine what it must have looked like before the disastrous fire as you wander around its dozens of apartments. St Michael's Church, which stands adjacent to the palace, is well worth a visit. The lane approaching the palace is lined with the crests of the monarchs of Britain.

Having said his goodbyes to Clementina Walkinshaw, Charles followed the Dumbarton Road west from Stirling. Hanoverian supporters had broken a hole in Stirling Bridge over the Forth which prevented the army from using it, so the road was taken to reach the bridge and fords at Frew that had been used on the march south. Charles halted for refreshment at Old Leckie before making the crossing.

That night the bulk of the army found quarters in the area between Doune and Dunblane. Charles rode on to spend the night near Crieff at Drummond Castle which stands entire to this day and is a private residence. (MAP A22) Its famous formal gardens are open to the public during the summer months.

On the 2nd the army moved forward to stay at Crieff and Perth, and Charles slept at Ferntower, a house belonging to the Drummond family. A council was held the next day when grievances rose to the surface. The army was obviously now in full retreat and the discussions turned to accusations. The rift between Charles and Lord George Murray began to widen when there was a disagreement

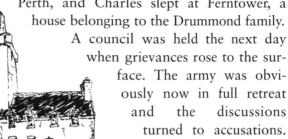

Drummond Castle

regarding which route of march to take. It was eventually decided that Charles would march north by the most direct route through the Highlands to Inverness, another section would take a more easterly route to reach Inverness from Speyside, and Lord George Murray would take a third contingent north by the coast road through Montrose and Aberdeen.

Charles remained at Ferntower till the morning of Tuesday 4 February, then he crossed the River Tay at Aberfeldy and halted at the far side at Castle Menzies at Weem where he stayed for two nights. His room is still pointed out. (The name Weem is a corrpution of the Gaelic *uaimh*, meaning cave.)

On the 6th he moved on to the castle at Blair Atholl. It was suggested that a stand could be made at Killiecrankie, to hold up the Hanoverian advance guard which was said to have reached Dunkeld. But Charles pointed out that the advance guard comprised many men from Clan Campbell who would be as familiar with hill warfare as his own men, and so the idea was abandoned.

While Charles remained at Blair, the bulk of his troops marched onward. They went by Dalnacandoch and Dalnaspidal, then up the ancient route through the Pass of Drumochter, which in February must have had a heavy covering of snow. Emerging at the far end of the pass at Dalwhinnie and following the route of the A9 through Glen Truim, the Highlanders soon arrived at Ruthven Barracks where an assault had been made on their road south.

Sergeant Mulloy, who had held off their earlier attack, had been promoted to lieutenant and was still in command. He was asked to surrender. Being no fool, and seeing the force that was arrayed against him, he capitulated. All members of the garrison were given a pass of safe conduct to allow them to return home, on condition that they promise not to bear arms against Charles for a period of two years. (Charles was always aware that the soldiers, whether on his side or the side of the Hanoverians, were his subjects.)

Charles left Blair Castle on 10 February. His officers asked him to set fire to the castle to make it unusable for the enemy, but Charles refused. Meanwhile, Cumberland had arrived at Crieff, where he let his men ravage the surrounding Drummond country. In a letter he wrote, 'I thought fit to let the soldiers a little loose, with proper precautions, that they might have some sweets with all their fatigues.'

Charles spent the nights of the 10th and 11th in the inn at Dalnacardoch and travelled through the Drumochter Pass on the 12th, spending the night at Dalwhinnie. On Thursday 13th he made contact with the main body at Ruthven, and he remained there, dwelling in a farmhouse for the next two nights. On the 15th some of the gunpowder found at Ruthven was used to destroy part of the building, and the army moved north to spend the night scattered in various houses and villages over the 20 miles or so between Aviemore and Moy. Charles took up quarters at Inverlaidnan House, several miles north-east of Aviemore, close to the Sluggan Bridge over the River Dulnain on one of General Wade's military roads. (MAP A23) By the late 1800s Inverlaidnan House was a ruin.

To visit Inverlaidnan today you follow the road running south-west following the River Dulnain from the centre of the village of Carrbridge. This road begins just south of the old 1715 bridge from which the village takes its name. After two and a half miles you can park and walk over the bridge across the river and up the private road, the ruins soon coming into sight. Inverlaid-nan was once a sizeable

Inverlaidnan House

property, but only one gable and some of the other walls still stand.

The following evening, Sunday the 16th, Charles transferred to Moy Hall, where a famous incident, The Rout of Moy, took place. (MAP A24) Lord Loudoun at Inverness received word that Charles was residing at Moy Hall, only some 10 miles south-east of Inverness itself, and a plan formed in his mind to capture him and win the government reward of £30,000. Around midnight, he left Inverness with a force of 1,500 men to effect Charles's capture. Lady Mackintosh, a staunch Jacobite residing in Inverness, had her suspicions aroused by the amount of activity amongst the Hanoverian troops, and sent a boy of fifteen, one Lauchlan MacIntosh, hot-foot to Moy to warn his Prince. Eventually he caught up with the marching soldiers, but in the rough country-side in the dark he could not overtake them or find a way to pass them on the road. By luck, when the soldiers came to a fork in the road, they took the longer route, the shorter one in very poor condition cutting over a wet moor. Lauchlan saw his chance and sprinted for Moy across the moor. He alerted Charles's bodyguard who roused him, and they moved south-west around Loch Moy to meet up with Locheil's regiment and safety.

Unknown to Charles, some two miles north of Moy the local

blacksmith, Donald Fraser, and four of his companions had taken up a position above the road that the Hanoverians had taken, at a corrie called Ciste Chraig an Eoin, purely as extra security to protect Charles. Ciste Chraig an Eoin stands about a mile and a half north of Moy on the old main route towards Inverness. Fraser's keen eyes saw the 1,500 Hanoverian troops approaching through the darkness in the early hours of the morning. His companions spread out, and when the troops came within musket-shot, the blacksmith fired, shouting 'Advance! advance! I think we have the dogs now!'. The four others fired their muskets, shouting various clan slogans. By chance, one of the leading Hanoverians was killed and the rest of the 1,500, thinking they had the whole Highland host before them, panicked and broke, sprinting back towards Inverness. They did not stop there, but abandoned the town to the Jacobites, moving north into Ross-shire, putting the Beauly Firth between themselves and their pursuers. At the end of his days the brave blacksmith was buried in the churchyard at Moy. His grave is marked by a pink granite pillar that was erected in 1903, marked 'The Captain of the Five'. Several descendants of the brave blacksmith are also interned within the little graveyard, which stands just cast of the 'old' A9, now superceded by a more modern stretch.

Moy Hall has seen many changes since that time. In the late 1800s it was reported that the library contained a sword said to have been presented to James V by the Pope, the sword worn by Bonnie Dundee at Killiecrankie, a sword of Charles I, and a gold watch that belonged to Mary Queen of Scots. A new Moy Hall was begun in 1955 to replace the older one which was damaged by fire. It is the seat of the chief of Clan Mackintosh.

From Moy, Charles and his men were able to march unopposed into Inverness on the 18th. Charles spent the night at Castlehill, a house two miles outside the town. The following day he moved to Culloden House, a mansion three miles east of

Inverness, where he met with Lord George Murray and the commanders of the other arms of the army that had taken the more easterly routes. The whole army was once again together.

A force was sent north to pursue Loudoun's men who had fled from Moy, but as the Hanoverians had been careful to take or destroy all available boats, this task was extremely difficult. Every time the Jacobites tried to come up with the Hanoverian forces by marching round the Beauly, Cromarty or Dornoch Firths, the Hanoverian forces simply crossed the water to the opposite bank and thwarted any attempts to bring them to battle.

It was decided that an attempt should be made to capture the castle at Inverness and attacks should be made on the Hanoverian barracks at Fort Augustus and Fort William. The next day, Thursday 20 February, rather unexpectedly the castle at Inverness was surrendered after only a few shots had been fired, and once the garrison left, Charles gave orders, probably prompted by local feeling, that the castle should be destroyed. (MAP A25) A French sergeant, l'Epine, who had some knowledge of explosives, blew up the towers of the castle in succession, but the last charge failed to detonate. L'Epine ran forward to ascertain the cause of the problem, but as he leaned over, the charge exploded, and he was blown into the air. His body was later recovered from the river.

A castle of one form or another has stood on the mound overlooking the River Ness for centuries. Kings of Scots have resided here from the time of MacBeth. The large baronial Gothic edifice which crowns the mound today contains the sheriff court house. You can stand here and look out over the river at the sprawl of modern Inverness and try to imagine the days when it was Inbhir Nis, and the hill was crowned with an early wooden fort – the days when St Columba first came here and Inverness was first mentioned in the earliest manuscripts. The museum at Inverness stands at the base of the north side of the castle mound and contains a wealth of Jacobite artefacts. No visitor should miss it. On the other side of the castle mound is a monument to the memory of Flora MacDonald who was to aid Charles during his later flight.

The assault on Fort Augustus began on 22 February. On 1 March a shell blew up the powder magazine and the garrison surrendered. The assault on Fort William then began, and continued in one form or another until 3 April when the Jacobites marched off, having come to see it as a lost cause.

Before the barracks were built, Fort Augustus was known as Cill-Cumin and Fort William was known as Inverlochy. In 1876 a Benedictine Abbey was built on the remains of Fort Augustus, and Fort William was dismantled after the last garrison left in 1855. It is a shame that Anglo-Saxon names have prevailed over the original Gaelic descriptions.

Monument to Flora MacDonald, Inverness

During this period, after staying at Culloden House, which is now a hotel, Charles took up quarters in a house in Kirk Street in Inverness. This house stood on the west side of the street and was demolished in 1843. Kirk Street is today known as Church Street.

On 11 March Charles set out for Gordon Castle, but became ill with 'an inflammation of the lungs', so he halted at Thunderton House in Batchen Lane in Elgin and remained there until he had recovered. After visiting Gordon Castle at Fochabers, much of which was demolished in 1955, Charles returned to his quarters in Kirk Street, and although details are vague, it would seem that he remained there until he left for Culloden on 4 April.

Cumberland set out from Aberdeen and came by way of Old Meldrum to Banff, then reached Cullen on 11 April. About noon on the 12th his forces came to the River Spey at Fochabers, to find a large force of Jacobites on the far bank under the command of the Duke of Perth. Cumberland split his army into three and ordered them to ford the river. The Jacobites could easily have attacked them as they crossed, or even have brought them to battle, with every chance of securing a victory. But the chance was lost. As the Hanoverians marched waist deep into the fast-flowing water, the Jacobites retired westward, much to Cumberland's surprise. Once across the Spey, his army made a straightforward march along the southern shores of the Moray Firth – and now the Hanoverians had much the upper hand in numbers.

CHAPTER 11

Culloden

ON THE NIGHT OF 13 APRIL Cumberland's army reached Alves, four miles west of Elgin. They reached Nairn the next day. The Hanoverians and Jacobites were now only 16 miles apart. In Inverness, Charles's men were preparing for the forthcoming battle. Culloden House was declared the rendezvous for the various detachments of the Jacobite army, and throughout the day many of the scattered regiments made their way there. Charles spent that night in Culloden House. (MAP A26) Next morning the Jacobites deployed in battle order, facing eastwards, about a mile south of the house, expecting Cumberland to approach from Nairn.

Lord George Murray had issued orders regarding the forthcoming battle. One line ran, 'It is His Royal Highness's positive orders that every person attach himself to some corps of the army, and remain with the corps night and day until the battle and pursuit be finally over.' A copy of this letter fell into Hanoverian hands, and it was doctored so that the line 'and to give no quarter to the Elector's (King George) troops on any account whatsoever' was inserted at the end. This was of course designed to give some justification to atrocities on the part of the Hanoverian army. Soldiers will show no mercy if they believe that their opponents will show none to them.

Word eventually filtered through that no attack would come that day. It turned out that 15 April was Cumberland's birthday, and he wished to celebrate it at Nairn with festivities for his troops.

A council of war was held by the Jacobite leadership. It was suggested that the army could quickly move south or west into more mountainous country where Cumberland's forces could be attacked easily, but dissenters pointed out that Cumberland would probably march straight to Inverness and capture the baggage train, so the idea was abandoned. It was then suggested that if Cumberland and his men were celebrating, it might be a good idea to launch an attack on them at Nairn in the middle of the night when it was least expected. This was agreed as an excellent plan. The Hanoverian troops would be under the effect of drink, and after their long retreat the Jacobites would not be expected to go on the offensive.

To avoid any news leaking to Cumberland of this intended attack, the ordinary rank and file of the Jacobite army were not informed of the plan. But there was a snag. The only ration that had been doled out that day was one biscuit to each man, and when the time came that evening for the army to stand down and camp for the night, 2,000 of them slipped away to forage for food. Their officers chased them, trying to cajole them into returning, but the men said they were starving and the officers could shoot them if they wanted, but they would not return till they had eaten.

The projected assault on Nairn was begun, however, the army again splitting into two, with Charles leading one half and Lord George Murray the other. For one reason or another, Lord George's section far outmarched Charles's, and Lord George later reported that he must have been asked to slow down or halt by runners fifty times in the first six miles.

The furthest point reached by the Jacobites was a farmhouse named Yellow Knowe on the Kilravock estate, some four miles short of Cumberland's camp. The horrible realisation dawned on them that they would not make the last stage in darkness, and they were far outnumbered. Lack of food was probably the reason for the sluggishness of Charles's section. The troops all staggered back, tired and hungry, to Culloden House, with men falling asleep by the roadside during the march. In the morning there was a rude awakening as runners brought the news that Cumberland was advancing towards them.

Some of the experienced soldiers in the army said that the Jacobites should cross the River Nairn towards Cumberland, where there was much broken ground which was more suitable for highland warfare, but others argued for the moor at Drummossie, south-east of Culloden House. The latter was chosen as the site of battle, for better or for worse, and the Highlanders drew up their battle lines. There was a stone wall on the Highlanders' right, as they faced east, which some saw as a screen, but Lord George Murray considered that this might afford shelter for enemy musketeers, and he wished to breach it by demolishing it in part. But time dictated that this was not done, as the Hanoverian advance guard were starting to appear in the distance.

The Jacobite forces comprised roughly 5,000 men. The Hanoverian forces, with some 8,000 men, divided into battle order, three lines marching west towards the Jacobite lines which were static but laid out in similar fashion.

It was bitterly cold, with a strong wind blowing from the east, carrying squalls of hail and snow into the face of the Highlanders. They had barely eaten for two days, and hunger coupled with the cold would have added to their low morale. Highlanders liked to be ready to fight in proper circumstances, when they could watch the enemy's approach, the adrenalin beginning to flow, creating the *crith gaisge*, or trembling of valour, the nervousness before the fight. As they went into combat, this was replaced by the *mire chath*, the frenzy of battle, a mad, slashing blood-lust that enveloped the spirit. But it must have been difficult to summon that kind of spirit as they watched the Hanoverian lines approach, the freezing sleet running from their hairlines into their eyes, and with hollow rumblings in their empty stomachs.

At 1pm on that fateful day, 16 April 1746, the two armies were in position on the moor, some 300 to 400 yards apart. The pipes of the Highlanders called out *'Thigibh an so! Clannabh nan con s'gheibh sibh feoil!'* – Come sons of dogs, and I will give you flesh! The cannon of both sides barked and shot flew across the field. Charles was determined that the Hanoverians should attack first, and for an hour the cannonade continued, Cumberland having very much the best of it. The Highland regiments fretted with inaction – this was not the way they fought, standing idle, targets for the opposing gunners. Every fibre of their being urged them to run with cold steel into the faces of their foes. But Charles did not give the order to charge. Charles's own groom, Thomas Ca, was decapitated by a cannonball, but still the Prince coolly sat upon his horse, watching the Hanoverian lines.

Cumberland, meanwhile, watched the movements of the Highlanders from the Cumberland Stone which stands a little to the east of the battlefield, or so the story goes. I find it hard to believe that someone as overweight as Cumberland would have been able to climb up onto such a large boulder. The boulder today has an inscription carved upon it, and iron rungs inserted to enable visitors to climb atop it. It stands a few hundred yards east of Culloden visitor centre, at the south side of the main road.

At last the order for the Jacobite advance was given, but before Lord George could give the word, the Mackintoshes, screaming their war cries, sprinted forward. Orders were given, and the Jacobite right wing – Frasers, Stewarts and Camerons – charged headlong towards the redcoated troops. Lord George Murray's earlier fears were realised with regard to the wall to the right of the Highland army. Hanoverian troops had sneaked up behind the cover of the dyke, and as the Highland right charged, they poured a withering fire into their ranks. Undaunted, the right smashed through the first lines of Hanoverians, slashing right and left, carving a way through, but the momentum faltered, and there was a second line standing ready to absorb the charge. The wave

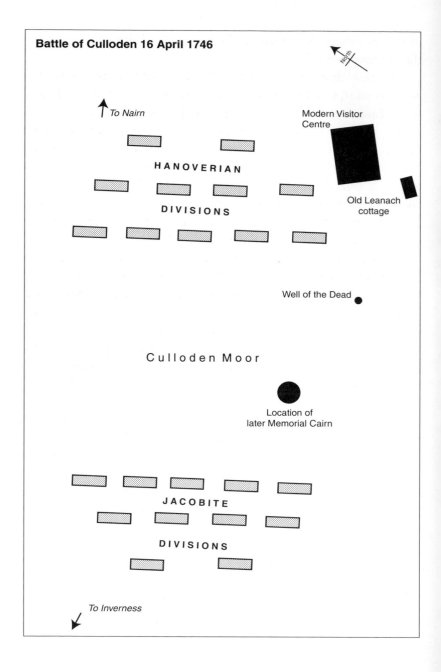

Battle of Culloden 16 April 1746

North

To Nairn

HANOVERIAN

DIVISIONS

Modern Visitor Centre

Old Leanach cottage

Well of the Dead

Culloden Moor

Location of later Memorial Cairn

JACOBITE

DIVISIONS

To Inverness

of tartan ebbed and broke on the bayonets of this second line on the Hanoverian left.

By this time the Jacobite left had charged in support – MacDonalds, Chisholms, MacLachlans, Macleods and MacLeans, but before contact with their opposite numbers in the Hanoverian ranks could be made through the cannon smoke and sleet, they saw their own right wing falling back in confusion after their failure to break the Hanoverian second line. This caused the onrush to waver, and the charge ground to a halt within 25 yards of the enemy. The Hanoverians were not slow to take advantage of this and poured volley after volley of grapeshot into the Jacobite left till the heather was dyed red with their blood.

Realisation dawned that the day was lost and won, and the Highlanders began to fall back, heading in the direction of Inverness, confused and disheartened. They did not know it at the time, but they were the lucky ones, as hundreds of their kinsmen were left dead on the heather. Even more unfortunate were the wounded, lying helpless with legs smashed with shot, for they were about to experience Cumberland's idea of the rules of warfare, the earlier tampering with the Jacobite orders having had its effect.

There were some astonishing acts of individual courage, however. Gillies MacBean killed fourteen men with his claymore as they tried to break through the wall on the Jacobite right before he succumbed to his wounds. The men of Appin fought bravely to try and prevent their banner from becoming a Hanoverian trophy, and no less than seventeen men were cut down, one after the other, trying to save it from dishonour. It was eventually borne to safety.

Grave at Culloden

There must be a hundred tales of horror and

valour connected with Culloden, all lost in the mists of time, but a hundred tales of courage do not make up for the great loss caused by such a vast military defeat, and we can only listen in sadness to the tale of Drumglass, pierced by many bayonet wounds, crawling to a little spring to get a last drink to allay his thirst. This spring still bubbles and is known today as the Well of the Dead.

Charles surveyed the carnage in a hypnotised state till two of his original companions who had landed with him in the Hebrides, Sheridan and O'Sullivan, grasped his horse's bridle and led him from the field.

When I first visited Culloden battlefield as a child, the place was covered in trees, woodland having engulfed the original moorland, but that didn't diminish my feelings when I discovered the scattered stones, standing here and there among the greenery, marking the last resting places of the clans. I was too young and naive to really appreciate what I was looking at, yet it did mean something deep inside. Being of Highland descent on both my mother's and father's side, perhaps the whole scene kindled some kind of race memory in me.

The battlefield is well signposted from the A9, and is crossed by the B9006. The trees have been cleared, taking the battle site back to the way that it looked in 1746. There is a modern visitor centre, with shop, cafe and audio-visual account of the battle, and

Old Leanach Cottage

I particularly like the collection of artefacts which includes swords and targes.

Beside the visitor centre is a little cottage named Leanach. It was in existence at the time of the battle, and some 30 or 40 wounded Highlanders crawled into it for refuge. They were discovered by Hanoverians, who fired the building, killing all within. A little further west is the Well of the Dead, and then you come across the first of the Highlanders' graves, clansman buried with clansman, standing around a large central cairn that was constructed as a monument in 1881. It bears a slab with the legend, 'The Battle of Culloden was fought on this moor, 16th April 1746. The graves of the gallant Highlanders who fought for Scotland and Prince Charlie are marked by the names of their clans.'

Cairn at Culloden

Modern flags have been raised to show the respective positions of the two armies at the onset of hostilities, red for Charles, yellow for Cumberland, and sign boards showing the positions of regiments have also been added. Walking the paths between the new growth of gorse and heather, you see the rising ground beyond the River Nairn to the south, and the blue expanse of the Moray Firth to the north and beyond it the Black Isle.

It is sad to have to acknowledge that a whole way of life came to an end on this field. The clan system with its tribal ways had its back broken here. Culloden was the end. Then it was the time of the Clearances, when sheep filled the glens of the men of the clans, regiments were raised by London governments to harness the fighting capacity of the Gael, and their blood helped to shade half the world in red on the maps. The Gaels benefitted the Anglo-

Saxons, as they were used to conquer foreign lands with which they themselves had no quarrel. Their dress was outlawed, the wearing of the kilt or plaid seen as an act of sedition. Boats were filled with Gaels and took them to scatter their seed all over the planet. It is incredible that the clan system survived as long as it did. After all, it operated only some 400 miles from the metropolis of London. It is difficult to imagine an equivalent race surviving in the 1700s within the same distance of other European capitals, such as Paris or Rome. Anything remotely different was usually regarded as savage by flourishing civilizations at that time, and seen as ripe for exploitation.

One point has always intrigued me. I remember reading of a

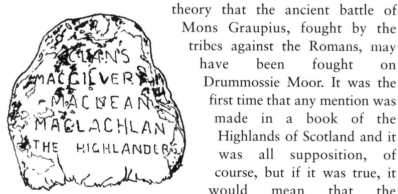

Grave at Culloden

theory that the ancient battle of Mons Graupius, fought by the tribes against the Romans, may have been fought on Drummossie Moor. It was the first time that any mention was made in a book of the Highlands of Scotland and it was all supposition, of course, but if it was true, it would mean that the Highlanders began with a battle on the same spot where centuries later a battle would mark the start of their demise.

When we look at Charles and what happened in the aftermath of Culloden, perhaps if he had died at Culloden he would have gone down in our history books as a martyr, and as a consequence would have been held in higher esteem by the Scots. His image has also been tarnished by his subsequent fall from grace in later years. Perhaps the treatment meted out to the people after Culloden would not have been so vindictive if the Hanoverians had not been so worried by the threat of his return. I don't know. What I do know is that Culloden battlefield has the power to move me, modern developments and tourism notwithstanding.

CHAPTER 12

Aftermath

THE SCOTS MAGAZINE IN their April 1746 edition carried an article penned by a Hanoverian officer. He stated, 'The moor was covered in blood, and our men, what with killing the enemy, dabbling their feet in the blood and splashing it about one another, looked like so many butchers.' From Culloden onwards, Cumberland gained the epithet The Butcher, or as the Highlanders would say, Am Feoladair. The little flower that took its name from Cumberland's victory was called Sweet William by a grateful London government, but it has since been known in Scotland as Stinking Billy.

General Hawley, the loser at Falkirk, was an evil man, and in his twisted mind he felt the need to exact revenge for his humiliation. It took the form of wholesale slaughter of all the wounded that were left on Culloden's field. Many Jacobites found alive were shot. Many of the wounded had their brains beaten out by musket butts. One woman travelling from Inverness to Moy reported seeing fourteen bodies of men, women and children on the road. The barbarity of the Hanoverian officers filtered down to the common ranks and they killed many innocent people in their thirst for vengeance.

Charles and a small group of companions took the route of the modern B851 which follows the river Nairn towards its source, then they went south-west through the country south of Loch Ness and the Great Glen. Charles resided that night at Gortuleg House. The next morning, the 17th, taking the route that the A862 follows, Charles's party reached the Great Glen and forded the River Oich at Aberchalder, then went along the north shore of

Loch Oich (the line of the modern A82) till they reached Invergarry Castle. (MAP D1) The castle was deserted, but a fishing net stretched out in the loch below had two salmon caught in it, and these provided them with supper.

Lord George Murray along with many fugitives, and whole parties who had missed the battle, began to arrive at Ruthven Barracks. It was expected that a fresh start to the campaign would be made. After all, the Jacobite forces had lost only one battle in the campaign. A sizeable force was soon gathered in the vicinity. They remained there till the 20th when a note arrived from Charles stating, 'Let every man seek his safety in the best way he can'. On receipt of this, the whole body of men began to disperse, some to the hills, some to ports where they hoped to sail to the continent, some back to their homes where they prayed they would be left in peace.

On the 18th Charles travelled the length of Loch Lochy, then turned west through the Mile Dorcha (The Dark Mile) to Loch Arkaig. The Dark Mile was so called because the thickness of the surrounding beech trees blocked out the light on the old track. (MAP D2) The newer road does not have the same quality, and the original beeches have been replaced by conifers. After travelling the length of Loch Arkaig, Charles spent the night in a cottage at Kinlocharkaig, having covered some 24 miles that day. The cottage now on the site replaces the original one which was burnt down around 1890.

The following day at around 5pm Charles set out with three companions through Glen Pean to Loch Morar, then covered the rough country on the roadless south side of that loch until Meoble was reached. The 19th was spent at Meoble, then on the 20th they walked across South Morar to Glen Beasdale near Borrodale, where he slept in a small cottage. Here he met some survivors of Culloden who spoke to him about resuming the struggle.

It seems that Charles had not at this point decided whether to continue the campaign or try and get a ship to return to France, but he had received a letter from Lord George Murray, a scathing note regarding the dispositions before Culloden, which ended with Lord George resigning his part in any future campaign. Perhaps this letter made Charles decide France would be the best option. He penned a farewell letter to be shown to the various chiefs who had supported him. It began, 'When I came into this country, it was my only view to do all in my power for your good and safety. This I will always do as long as life is in me. But alas! I see with grief I can at present do little for you on this side of the water ...'

Charles had strong hopes of persuading the king of France to mount an invasion, and after the carnage of Culloden he had no illusions about the horrors the Hanoverian regime would inflict on his sympathisers. He knew the only way forward was to reach France, then return with French troops and save his friends in Scotland – and this time elicit success in his quest for the throne.

He remained at Glen Beasdale till Saturday 26 April, when he set sail from Borrodale for the Outer Isles in a fishing boat, powered by eight oarsmen. One of the rowers, Murdoch MacLeod, was only fifteen. He was at school at Inverness when he heard of the imminent battle at Culloden, and had armed himself with a claymore, dirk and pistol and had taken part in the battle before fleeing westwards and meeting up with the fugitive Charles.

The journey to Benbecula was a nightmare, a horrific storm blowing and Charles heavily seasick. Incredibly, they covered the 70 miles from Loch nan Uamh to Benbecula in one night despite the atrocious weather. Out in the storm-tossed Minch Charles said, 'I had rather face cannons and muskets than be drowned in such a storm as this.'

Landing on Benbecula on 27 April, Charles was to spend the next two months in the Outer Hebrides, often hungry and in situations of extreme discomfort, with a price of £30,000 on his head. The Hanoverians needed him in person to seal their victory over the forces of Jacobitism, but Charles was made of stern stuff, and handled all his torments with little complaint.

The first night was spent in a hut at Rossinish, and on the 28th they took to the sea again, rowing northwards and landing on the island of Scalpay at the mouth of Loch Seaforth on the island of Lewis. One of the Prince's companions, Donald MacLeod, went on to Stornoway to charter a boat to take Charles to France – and succeeded, hiring a brig of forty tons for £100. But the rumour that Charles might be in these parts had already reached the islands, and the captain grew suspicious and reneged on the deal.

The Reverend MacAuley, the minister of Harris and an ardent Hanoverian, actually made an attempt to capture Charles at this time, but failed. During the five months of the Prince's life as a fugitive after Culloden, this was the only occasion that someone tried to claim the reward money for his capture. The inhabitants of the Highlands and islands of Scotland were in the main a poor people, but they had a finely attuned sense of what was right and wrong, a strong sense of duty in conduct concerning hospitality, and none would have what they saw as blood money staining their hands.

Charles and his companions sailed to the most northern reach of Loch Seaforth, in the hope that a ship had been chartered, and started to walk to Stornoway. The night was wet and stormy, and it took them 18 hours and 36 miles of walking over sodden boggy moors before the town came into view. (MAP D3) They lodged at Kildun House in Arnish, only to find that the hoped for chartered boat was not available.

On 6 May Charles was rowed south, heading back to Scalpay, but English frigates searching for him were spotted, and a landing was made at the little island of Iubhard at the mouth of Loch Shell. For four days they remained there, sheltering in a tiny hut. Taking to sea again, the next stop was a small island in Loch Uskavagh in Benbecula, where again their refuge was a hut. The next stop was on South Uist, where shelter was found above an inlet on the coast, between the island's two highest hills, Ben More at 2,034 feet and Hecla at 1,988 feet. A cave is pointed out as Charles's refuge, but his companions later stated that they sheltered in a hut at Carradale. (MAP D4) Charles remained here for three weeks, and his skill with weapons enabled him to kill grouse and deer enough to feed them all. In this time of respite, when trusted souls managed to bring them some luxuries, it was reported that during drinking sessions, Charles would still be fresh when his companions had succumbed to drunken slumber. Charles had a resistance to the effects of alcohol that allowed him to keep drinking when his companions had had enough. But his continued hard drinking was to take its toll on his health in later years.

Charles was a pipe smoker, and he showed his companions how to lengthen their broken clay pipes with the quill of a seabird's feather, which also gave a cooler smoke. When one of his companions complained of losing a shoe, Charles laughed and displayed the bottom of one of his own which had lost its sole.

Unknown to the fugitives, two French ships had arrived in Arisaig. If he had not sailed to the Outer Isles, Charles could have been plucked to safety much earlier than he eventually was. The ships landed 40,000 Louis d'or (gold coins) to finance Charles's war-chest. These coins were ferried by boat up Loch Morar, carried through Glen Pean to Loch Arkaig side, and were supposedly buried there. A few optimistic searchers believe that they may still be buried in the area, but I'm sure the clansmen who carried them here would not be slow in recognising an opportunity once the rising had failed.

Hanoverian ships gathered in the Minch in ever increasing numbers, landing red-coated soldiers on the islands to conduct thorough searches. Between the 5th and the 21st of June Charles was shuttled up and down the coast to various hiding places, some no more than clefts in rocks. Many caves on the eastern seaboard of South Uist and Benbecula are pointed out as refuges.

It was only a matter of time till the government search parties closed in, and it is at this point that a famous name enters the story. Fionnghal MacDonald, better known as Flora, has gone down in history books as a heroine, her story intertwined with that of Charles. She was born at Milton on South Uist in 1722 and was descended from the chiefs of Clanranald. (MAP D5) She was reported as 'not tall, but well proportioned', and had attended school in Edinburgh, mixing with polite society, and so she had experience of city life and would have been familiar with the politics of the time from

Cairn marking Flora MacDonald's birthplace

every angle. Flora was well connected, and managed to obtain a pass for herself and a maid to cross the Minch to Skye where she had family. Charles was duly disguised as the maid under the name of Betty Burke. He wished to wear a pistol under his petticoat, but Flora objected, saying its discovery would give them away. Charles replied, 'Indeed, miss, if we shall happen with any that will go so narrowly to work in searching me as what you mean, they will certainly discover me at any rate.'

They set sail on 28 June from Loch Uskavagh in North Uist, Charles keeping guard over the sleeping Flora, scared that one of the oarsmen might tread upon her. It was this journey eastwards that inspired the song 'Over the Sea to Skye', although the popular misconception still exists in the imagination of Scots that this song commemorates a journey from the mainland westwards to Skye. (MAP D6)

They first made a short stop on the Vaternish peninsula of

Skye to rest the crew who had been rowing against a contrary wind, then they rounded the top of that peninsula where they ignored shouts from a couple of sentries to 'pull in'. The broad Loch Snizort was crossed and they landed just north of Kilbride where a burn cuts over the beach. It was 2pm on the 29th.

A long walk to Kingsburgh further south on the coast then awaited Charles before he could rest for the night. He was still in female apparel, and drew stares from all he passed on the road. The lady of the house at Kingsburgh was taken aback at his appearance, not guessing her visitor's identity, and stated to her husband, 'What a long odd hussie was this he had brought to the house?' and 'she made such lang wide steps through the hall that I could not like her appearance at all'. (MAP D7) Nothing now remains of the house at Kingsburgh, although the name lives on on modern maps showing the site.

After sleeping in a bed for the first time since April at Culloden, Charles set out with Flora for Portree on the 30th, discarding his female attire in a wood and donning a plaid and broadsword. He met up with friends in an inn at Portree where the locals took it that he was a Highland gentleman, probably down on his luck after Culloden as so many were at that time. Charles had spent so much time in the wilds that he probably looked no different than the average Highlander, and he had taken a soaking on the way to Portree. He remained in the inn till the morning of 1 July, when he embarked upon a waiting boat and headed east for Raasay. He bade farewell to Flora MacDonald, saying, 'Madam, we shall meet at St James's yet', referring to St James's Palace in London. But they never met again.

Raasay was no place for Charles to hide. It had already been visited by the Hanoverians, and like so much of the Highlands, had been devastated. Every house was burnt, every animal found had been slaughtered and left on the heather to rot, one man had been beaten to death, and several women were raped, including a blind girl and a woman 'who walked upon stilts'. Due to the situation on the island, Charles spent only one night on Raasay in a hut at Glam, heading back across to Skye on the 2nd and landing at Scorobreck, two miles north of Portree. That night was spent in a little byre.

The following day Charles went for a walk, accompanied by one companion. Knowing the ground they walked intimately, I have real admiration for the distance covered in this single excursion. They left the byre north of Portree, and skirting the town to the west, walked along Glen Varragill south to Sligachan, which was also skirted. They then crossed the high ground of the Red Cuillins, traversing between Marsco and Ben Dearg, only to turn again to circle Loch Ainort before walking down Strath Mor. Reaching Loch Slapin, they walked under Blaven's rocky heights, then followed the line of the modern A881 to Elgol on Loch Scavaig. It was a walk of 12 hours and some 30 miles covered. Many modern-day walkers with the best of equipment would be daunted by such a trek. Charles and his companion drank a bottle of brandy on the last stretch, and it is possible they walked barefoot. On top of this it was discovered that Charles was infested with lice, and his companion picked 80 off his body before they spent the night at Elgol. (MAP D8)

The following evening Charles was rowed back to mainland Scotland, landing in the early hours of 5 July at Mallaigvaig (or Mallaig Beag – little Mallaig), just north-east of Mallaig. For the next three nights they slept out in the open on the hillsides – luckily it was now the highland summer. On the 8th Charles moved south, fording the River Morar at the famous silver sands, hoping to find shelter at the house of Cross, a MacDonald property, but the house had been burnt. Charles spent the night in a cave instead, in a cliff at Scamadale on Loch Morar side.

The next day he crossed the Mointeach Mor, a large peat moor, and travelled the five miles south-east to Borrodale House where he had stayed soon after arriving in Scotland. But it too was a blackened, burnt-out shell. The owner was residing in a cave down by the shore which is marked on Ordnance Survey maps as 'Prince Charles's Cave', and Charles slept here for three nights.

Next he occupied a cave four miles to the east of Borrodale, but ships could be seen gathering out in the Sound of Arisaig, and a move was made north-east over Beinn nan Cabar to Meoble. Charles had been here after Culloden. After a night at Meoble, word came that there was a cordon of Redcoats around the whole district, and to avoid them a route was taken by Loch Beoraid, and Charles climbed up and spent a night on the summit of Sgurr Thuilm (3,164ft), at the head of Glen Finnan, making him an early Munroist. (MAP D9)

It must have been a strange experience for him, as just a few miles south was the spot where his standard was raised only the year before. Much had changed since then. To climb this mountain and look at the view that Charles saw, you can park at the village of Glenfinnan and walk up the left bank of the river to the base of the hill. The climb is rough going. The famous Rough Bounds of Knoydart are not too far north from here, and some of that description certainly applies to these hills.

Leaving Sgurr Thuilm on the evening of the 19th, they discovered that there were camps of Hanoverian troops spread out to their north and east, stationed at half-mile intervals, with fires lit at night as they kept watch for any who might try to pass in the dark. At about 2pm on the 20th a halt was made, and Charles hid in a crevice in Meall an Spardan above Loch Quoich. The following evening they managed to slip by one of the enemy fires and outposts in Gleann Cosaidh. Moving quickly, the small party climbed the hill opposite, but near the summit Charles slipped while crossing the channel of a burn and almost fell into the abyss beyond. The quick response of one of his companions saved him, however, as he managed to grasp hold of Charles as he fell.

They followed the ridge of Sgurr nan Chlaideimh, travelling north-east, then dropped to ford the river a little east of Kinlochhourn. Just before daybreak on the 21st they reached Coire Sgoir-adail where they could rest. That night they crossed the Bealach Dubh Leac into Glen Shiel. It was only some five miles, but it was hard and rough going. Dropping into Glen Shiel they were now in territory more familiar to most people today, Glen Shiel being traversed by the modern A87 that runs from the Great Glen to Kyle of Lochalsh and Skye. Although the glen was crossed by one of General Wade's military roads, the scenery is on a grand scale, and cover was available for men determined to hide.

CHAPTER 13

Further Wanderings

SPENDING 22 AND 23 JULY traversing the length of Glen Shiel in an easterly direction, it was reported that Charles suffered greatly from midge bites. Having been coated with these fiends several times myself during mountain forays, I can only feel sympathy for Charles, dressed in a plaid, with much flesh showing for them to feast upon.

Eventually they turned due north at Loch Clunie and ascended Sgurr nan Conbhairean. Here Charles met a group of refugees from Culloden whose name has gone down in history as The Seven Men of Glenmoriston. (MAP D10) These men had taken an oath 'never to yield to Cumberland, but to die on the spot, never to give up their arms, and that for all the days of their lives', and this with some reason. They had seen their cattle slaughtered, their houses burned, even their friends murdered. They based themselves in a cave at the head of Coire Sgrainge, and sallied out to kill small groups of Hanoverians and informers. One they had captured was decapitated and his head was hung near the garrison at Fort Augustus as a warning to others.

There is another Charles connection in this area. In Glen Moriston, where the river Doe meets the river Moriston, stands a memorial to Roderick Mackenzie. Roderick was of similar looks and build to Charles, and when he was shot by pursuing Redcoats, he exclaimed, 'You have slain your Prince!' The Redcoats did indeed believe that they had slain Charles, and as a consequence the Prince gained a few days' respite from pursuit. Opposite the memorial stands a wooden cross which is said to be the site of Mackenzie's grave.

The Seven Men were shocked to see Charles in such a poor state. He remained at their cave until the 28th when a move was made to another shelter formed by a fall of rocks from the cliffs of Tigh Mor at the head of Coire Mheadhain.

On 1 August, hearing that Hanoverian soldiers were near at hand, they travelled north-east to Strath Glass where Charles skulked for the next ten days. (MAP D11) There had been word that French ships had been sighted at Loch Ewe, and trusted individuals were sent off to see if this information could be substantiated. Word was received that French officers were searching for Charles at Loch Arkaig, 25 miles south. They reached there on the morning of 15 August, having slept in the open each night, often in torrential rain.

A description of Charles around this time says, 'He was barefooted, had an old black kilt coat on, a plaid, philabeg (little kilt) and waistcoat, a dirty shirt and a long red beard, a gun in his hand, a pistol and dirk by his side. He was very cheerful and in good health.' He continued to hide in the Arkaig area till 28 August. A tree in the Dark Mile, east of Loch Arkaig, was called the Prince's Tree. It was an old, hollow tree, and it is said that Charles hid inside it from the searching troops.

Roderick Mackenzie plaque

At this point he decided to travel right across the Highlands to Badenoch to meet up with two of his former officers, Locheil and Cluny MacPherson, who were hiding out at Ben Alder. The 28th was spent travelling across the River Lochy at Mucomer and following the east side of Loch Lochy and Loch Oich. Then, moving south near the Corrieyairach, they crossed high Creag Meaghaidh and then rounded Loch Laggan. After resting at Coire an Iubhair, they continued to Ben Alder on the morning of the 29th. It had been a journey of more than 40 miles across rough country and over mountaintops, and the Highlanders accompanying Charles were so impressed with his stamina that one remarked, 'Show me a king or prince in Europe that could have done a tenth part of it'.

Charles met up with Locheil and Cluny MacPherson, spending a couple of nights in huts in the area, then on 5 September they all moved to Cluny's Cage. (MAP D12) Its exact location is open to debate, although its site has been marked confidently on old maps. It was constructed of turf, stood two floors in height and was built against a slab of rock that hid any smoke from its cooking fires. Charles had been living here for a week, in much greater comfort than in many habitations so far, when word came that there were some French vessels at Loch nan Uamh where he had landed fourteen months earlier. Although this news arrived around 1 am on 13 September, nothing would do but for Charles to make an immediate start for the loch, far to the north-west, to discover the truth for himself. He still believed that the French would assist him with all the aid that he required.

The first halt was made at a bothy named Uisge Chaoil Reidhe. Charles saw one of his officers, Colonel John Roy Stuart, approaching the bothy. The colonel did not know Charles was inside, and when he entered, Charles suddenly stuck his head out from under the plaid where he had been hiding. The Colonel was so shocked to see his prince that he fainted, dropping into a pool of water, which caused much hilarity in the small company.

When it grew dark, they travelled north between Ben Alder and Loch Ericht, then turned west through Ben Alder forest, fording the River Spean at the south end of Loch Laggan. The next day was spent in the corrie of the Moy burn, above Moy on the modern A86. After they had slept, they had a shooting contest, firing their

pistols at a bonnet thrown up in the air. Charles, excellent marks-
man that he was, easily won.

On the evening of the 14th they set off again and came down
the glen of the Glas Dhoire burn into Glen Roy the morning of the
next day. They managed to cross the River Lochy in a leaky boat
that the Hanoverians had missed when destroying property in the
area. The 16th was spent at Achnacarry, Locheil's destroyed property, and the following night was spent traversing the south shore
of Loch Arkaig, now very familiar to Charles, where provisions
awaited them.

They continued by Glen Camgharaidh, which runs south-west
from Loch Arkaig, and again passed close to Glenfinnan. They
reached Borrodale on the 19th and there in Loch nan Uamh lay
two French ships, *L'Heureux* and *Prince de Contie*. (MAP D13)

In the early hours of Saturday 20 September Charles boarded
L'Heureux with many of the officers who had
fought with him at Culloden. They set sail in
the belief that they would soon return with
French aid and the Stuarts would again
sit upon the throne, but
Charles was never to
return. The people of
the Highlands awaited
his coming in vain.
Their sorrow echoed in
the words of many songs in
years to come. Stories of
Charlie are still handed
down in various districts in the

Loch nan Uamh cairn

Highlands. Even after the carnage of Culloden
and its aftermath, the people would still sing 'Will ye no come back
again?' Perhaps the Highland ideal of loyalty was to prove to be
their ultimate undoing.

As Charles stood on the rolling deck of *L'Heureux* as it sailed out into the swell of the open sea, what went through his head when he looked back to the landscape of Scotland growing fainter behind him? A cairn with a plaque marks the spot where Charles climbed aboard the rowing boat that took him out to the waiting ships. It was erected in 1956 by the '45 Association and stands beside the A830. You can park in a lay-by just west of the spot. Loch nan Uamh is completely unspoilt, and you look out over its islet-dotted surface as

A RÉIR BEUL-AITHRIS IS ANN BHO 'N TRÀIGH SO A SHEÒL AM PRIONNSA TEARLACH AIR AIS DO 'N FHRAING

THIS CAIRN MARKS THE TRADITIONAL SPOT FROM WHICH PRINCE CHARLES EDWARD STUART EMBARKED FOR FRANCE 20ᵀᴴ SEPTEMBER 1746.

ERECTED BY THE FORTY-FIVE ASSOCIATION 1956

Plaque on cairn at Loch Nan Vamh

Charles did in 1746. He had grown to know the countryside north of here during his long wanderings as well as any native. But the emptiness of the landscape today is a lasting testament to the failure of the '45, and the descendants of that time are now scattered over the face of the earth.

CHAPTER 14

Later Years

FLORA MACDONALD WAS ARRESTED soon after taking leave of Charles and was taken aboard the sloop *Furnace*. She was held in Dunstaffnage Castle on Loch Etive, then after a few days was transferred to Glasgow and then to Leith, where she was put on board a ship to be taken to London. Word that she had smuggled Charles away from the clutches of the Hanoverians had spread far and wide, and thousands gathered at Leith to watch her depart.

She was kept prisoner for a while in the Tower of London, then allowed to stay under a restraint order in the house of an official. After a year she was given her freedom and was told she could return to Scotland. However, she was by now regarded as the doyen of London society and for a while she attended party after party, but she always longed to go home to the heather-clad hills and moors and the vast skies of the islands. On her return she discovered that she was as feted in Scotland as she was in London. She was married in November 1750 to a son of one of Charles's supporters. They emigrated to North Carolina, but returned to Skye when the American War of Independence broke out. Flora died in 1790. She lies in the graveyard at Kilmuir in Skye, four miles north of Uig, not far from the spot where she landed with Charles after the crossing from the Outer Isles. (MAP D14) Her grave is marked by an

Flora MacDonald's grave

Iona cross of Aberdeen granite 28.5ft high, erected in 1880. It replaced one built in 1871 which was blown down and broken in a gale in December 1873.

Lord George Murray who acted as second in command throughout the whole of the campaign of 1745-46 disappeared after the dispersal at Ruthven, and the next mention of his whereabouts is Holland in December 1746. He travelled across Europe to Rome, arriving in March 1747. He tried to make contact with Charles, but Charles refused to see him. He felt enmity towards Lord George even though everyone around Charles tried to convince him that Lord George had only his best interests at heart. Lord George never approached Charles again, and he died at Medemblik, North Holland, on 11 October 1760, aged 66. He was interred under the choir of the Reformed Church there.

Many of the officers who served Charles were captured and taken south for show trials and execution, most notably Lord Kilmarnock and Lord Balmerino. Lord Lovat, almost 80, was beheaded. Many other noblemen were exiled. With regard to the clansmen, hundreds were sold as slaves and transported to the plantations. The Americas are littered with Jacobite graveyards filled with headstones showing places of birth like Balquidder, Perthshire, or Isle of Skye or Glen Etive – people who knew the sharp tang of highland air, now buried in lands of tropical heat. Even their language declined sharply, speakers of the Gaelic tongue scattered like chaff in the wind.

> From the lone shieling on the misty island
> Mountains divide us and the waste of the sea
> Yet still the blood is strong, the heart is highland,
> And we in dreams behold the Hebrides.

There were some happier events, however. For example, there is a spot above the Devil's Beeftub, a mighty hollow north of Moffat at the source of the River Annan, which is known as

MacCleran's Loup. This MacCleran, or more probably MacLaren, was a Jacobite prisoner being taken south to be executed. While being marched along the edge of the Beeftub, on the line of the modern A701, he saw his chance to escape and threw himself over the edge of the precipice. Rolled up in his plaid like a hedgehog, he tumbled down into the misty depths, luckily missing the flurry of musket shot that followed, and made a complete getaway. A stone marks the spot.

Charles arrived at Roscoff in Brittany on 10 October 1746. He was reunited with his brother, Henry Benedict, and quarters were provided for him in Paris at the Chateau de St Antoine. He managed to speak to the French king on 21 October at Fontainebleau, but the king shied away from speaking of the situation in Scotland. Over the next year Charles realised that there was a deliberate coolness in discussing mounting another attempt to regain his, or rather his father's, throne. It is said that he was approached by a diplomat who inquired tentatively whether Charles would be interested in ceding Ireland to France if a successful invasion of the British Isles took place. Charles would not hear of such a suggestion. It is a strange situation to consider. What would the Irish have felt about being handed over to French rule?

Charles apparently felt acute embarrassment at the fact that he had told the chiefs of Scotland that he would return with French aid and now seemed to be helpless. He travelled to Madrid to try to elicit aid from Spain, arriving there on 2 March 1747, but he was met with a similar disinterest to that in France.

The Stuart cause received a blow in April 1747 when news came that Henry, Charles's brother, had become a Cardinal of the Church of Rome. This effectively put paid to any claim that Henry had to the throne of Scotland and England, and as he was next in line after James and Charles, we can imagine King George and his supporters rubbing their hands in glee. Charles was very aware that his Catholicism was a major drawback to his ascending the throne. He had made it clear to even his most hardened enemies that he was in favour of religious freedom, but he felt that his brother's donning of the scarlet hat of a Cardinal might prove a diplomatic weapon for his enemies to wield. Henry, however, was of a different temperament to Charles, and his religious calling was very strong.

In 1748 the French king began to tire of having Charles in Paris, even though he was obviously popular with the citizens, and he was asked to leave. Charles continued with his daily life but one night on his way to the opera he was arrested, bound with silken cords and escorted from French soil. He arrived in Avignon which was then under the jurisdiction of the Vatican. When the Hanoverian government was informed of his whereabouts, they threatened to bombard the town if Charles was not expelled.

He wandered Europe for a while, residing in various cities, and then, surprisingly, he made plans to visit London. He had landed in Scotland in 1745 with very little backing, and now that he could get no aid from the crowned heads of Europe, he again made a solo effort. Certainly, he sailed from Antwerp and spent perhaps a week in London in September 1750. There is a plaque on a building in Essex Street, just off the Strand in London, which mentions Charles visiting a building there but gives no other detail.

ESSEX STREET
was laid out in the grounds
of Essex House by
NICHOLAS BARBON in 1675
Among many famous lawyers
who lived here were
Sir ORLANDO BRIDGEMAN c.1606-1674
Lord Keeper.
HENRY FIELDING 1707-1754
Novelist and
BRASS CROSBY 1725-1793
Lord Mayor of London
JAMES SAVAGE 1779-1852 Architect
had his office here.
PRINCE CHARLES EDWARD STUART
stayed at a house in the street
in 1750
Rev. THEOPHILUS LINDSEY 1723-1808
Unitarian Minister
founded Essex Street Chapel here
in 1774
Dr. SAMUEL JOHNSON
established an evening club at
the Essex Head in 1783

Essex St. plaque, London

It was believed a plot had been hatched to overthrow the House of Hanover, and Charles was determined to find out as much about this as possible. But on his arrival in London he found again that English Jacobitism was much more lukewarm than had been reported, and however loudly his supporters in England espoused his cause, their actions were not of the same calibre as their words.

A surprising revelation from the London visit is that Charles later announced he had embraced the Protestant faith as taught by the Anglican Church while he was there. It is believed this conversion took place at the church of St Mary's-le-Strand which still stands in the city. Charles remained a Protestant for most of the rest of his life, only converting back to Roman Catholicism shortly before he died.

On his return to the continent Charles drifted in and out of obscurity. Clementina Walkinshaw with whom he had started a relationship in Scotland reappeared on the scene. She made contact with Charles and they set up home together in Liege. In 1753 she bore Charles a daughter who was christened Charlotte. The relationship between Charles and Clementina lasted till 1760, when they parted, never to meet again. Bitterness over the cards that life had dealt him now came to the fore. He turned ever more to alcohol and found solace in its oblivion. It took its toll, and Charles was no longer the fit young man who had lived life so energetically in Scotland.

His father, James VIII and III, died on New Year's Day 1766 and was buried at St Peter's in Rome. Charles was now regarded by the Jacobites as King Charles III.

St Mary's-le-Strand

He was by this time residing in the Frascati area of Italy, and his brother Henry is reported talking about Charles's dependence on 'the nasty bottle'.

Charles married again on 17 April 1772. His bride was

Princess Louisa Maximiliana Emmanuela of Stolberg, a girl of nineteen. She was born at Mons in September 1752, seven years after the Battle of Culloden. The marriage was a grievous mistake, and it soon broke down irreconcilably. There were no children from the marriage, although later pretenders have made claims to be descendants of this union.

About three years before his death, Charles was reunited with his daughter Charlotte. She did her best to look after him during his twilight years, and she reported that any reference to Scotland greatly upset her father. On one occasion when Charles had a visitor, Charlotte entered the room to find him in a convulsive state. She berated the visitor for 'speaking to my father about Scotland and the Highlanders'.

In 1787 Charles returned to the house in Rome in which he was born, the Palazzo Muti in the Square of the Santi Apostoli. He suffered a stroke and died on the morning of 31 January 1788. It is strange that the building where Charles was born, a birth that was believed to be an omen of the resurgence of Stuart fortunes, should also be the place where he breathed his last. The Palazzo today is coloured yellow, and is little changed since Charles's time. It bears a plaque in its carriage entrance testifying to its connection with the Stuarts.

The Pope would not allow Charles to be buried at the Vatican, so he was interred in the church at Frascati, the royal emblems of crown, sceptre and sword laid upon his coffin. His brother, now regarded as Henry ix and i, presided over the funeral. Charlotte only outlived her father by a year. She died in 1789 from an abscess in her side caused by a fall from a horse.

Henry outlived Charles by nineteen years, dying on 13 July 1807. As a Cardinal, he was given a magnificent funeral at St Peter's in Rome. Charles's remains were secretly conveyed from Frascati, and the two coffins were placed in the vault of the crypt called the Old Grotto beside that of their father, James.

Twelve years later, Pope Pius VII commissioned a monument, sculpted by Canova and bearing likenesses of the three, to be raised in St Peter's. In 1939 the tomb was opened and their bodies were placed in new coffins and a magnificent tomb of red Travertine marble was erected above them in the crypt.

Tomb in St Peter's

* * *

Many artefacts survive from the fourteen months Charles spent in these islands. The museums have large collections of weapons, glasses and even suits of clothes from those times. Locks of Charles's hair and strips of tartan from his clothing have been passed down through families and are treasured mementoes. Even the recipe of the alcoholic drink Drambuie is said to have been one of Charles's legacies, having been passed on in gratitude for services rendered. Enough time has elapsed for the very real human suffering caused by the '45 to be partially obscured by rose-tinted romance. It is now a piece of the fabric of Scotland's history, one bit of the pattern in the rich tartan that comprises the ongoing story of Scotland. Long may it continue!

Bibliography

Ordnance Gazetteer of Scotland
(William MacKenzie, 1893)

The Topographical, Statistical and Historial
Gazetteer of Scotland
(A. Fullarton & Co., Glasgow, 1842)

AA Illustrated Road Book of Scotland
(The Automobile Association, London,
1969)

Culloden, The Swords and The Sorrows
(National Trust for Scotland, 1996)

LINKLATER, Eric   The Prince in the Heather
(Hodder and Stoughton Ltd., London 1965)

MUNRO, R.W.   Highland Clans and Tartans
(Peerage Books, London, 1987)

MURRAY, W.H.   The Companion Guide to the West
Highlands of Scotland
(Collins, London, 1968)

NORIE, W. Drummond   The Life and Adventures of Prince Charles
Edward Stuart, Four Volumes
(The Caxton Publishing Company,
London, 1900)

SALTER, Mike   The Castles of Scotland Series, Five Volumes
(Folly Publications, Worcester, 1994)

TRANTER, Nigel   The Fortified House in Scotland, Five
Volumes
(The Mercat Press, Edinburgh, 1986)

Some other books published by **LUATH** PRESS

ON THE TRAIL OF

On the Trail of William Wallace

David R. Ross

ISBN 0 946487 47 2 PBK £7.99

How close to reality was *Braveheart*?

Where was Wallace actually born?

What was the relationship between Wallace and Bruce?

Are there any surviving eye-witness accounts of Wallace?

How does Wallace influence the psyche of today's Scots?

On the Trail of William Wallace offers a refreshing insight into the life and heritage of the great Scots hero whose proud story is at the very heart of what it means to be Scottish. Not concentrating simply on the hard historical facts of Wallace's life, the book also takes into account the real significance of Wallace and his effect on the ordinary Scot through the ages, manifested in the many sites where his memory is marked.

In trying to piece together the jigsaw of the reality of Wallace's life, David Ross weaves a subtle flow of new information with his own observations. His engaging, thoughtful and at times amusing narrative reads with the ease of a historical novel, complete with all the intrigue, treachery and romance required to hold the attention of the casual reader and still entice the more knowledgable historian.

74 places to visit in Scotland and the north of England

One general map and 3 location maps

Stirling and Falkirk battle plans

Wallace's route through London

Chapter on Wallace connections in North America and elsewhere

Reproductions of rarely seen illustrations

On the Trail of William Wallace will be enjoyed by anyone with an interest in Scotland, from the passing tourist to the most fervent nationalist. It is an encyclopaedia-cum-guide book, literally stuffed with fascinating titbits not usually on offer in the conventional history book.

David Ross is organiser of and historical

adviser to the Society of William Wallace.

'*Historians seem to think all there is to be known about Wallace has already been uncovered. Mr Ross has proved that Wallace studies are in fact in their infancy.*' ELSPETH KING, Director the the Stirling Smith Art Museum & Gallery, who annotated and introduced the recent Luath edition of *Blind Harry's Wallace.*

'*Better the pen than the sword!*'
RANDALL WALLACE, author of *Braveheart*, when asked by David Ross how it felt to be partly responsible for the freedom of a nation following the Devolution Referendum.

On the Trail of Robert the Bruce

David R. Ross

ISBN 0 946487 52 9 PBK £7.99

On the Trail of Robert the Bruce charts the story of Scotland's hero-king from his boyhood, through his days of indecision as Scotland suffered under the English yoke, to his assumption of the crown exactly six months after the death of William Wallace. Here is the astonishing blow by blow account of how, against fearful odds, Bruce led the Scots to win their greatest ever victory. Bannockburn was not the end of the story. The war against English oppression lasted another fourteen years. Bruce lived just long enough to see his dreams of an independent Scotland come to fruition in 1328 with the signing of the Treaty of Edinburgh. The trail takes us to Bruce sites in Scotland, many of the little known and forgotten battle sites in northern England, and as far afield as the Bruce monuments in Andalusia and Jerusalem.

67 places to visit in Scotland and elsewhere.

One general map, 3 location maps and a map of Bruce-connected sites in Ireland.

Bannockburn battle plan.

Drawings and reproductions of rarely seen illustrations.

On the Trail of Robert the Bruce is not all blood and gore. It brings out the love and laughter, pain and passion of one of the great eras of Scottish history. Read it and you will understand why David Ross has never knowingly killed a spider in his life. Once again, he proves himself a master of the popular brand of hands-on history that made *On the Trail of William Wallace* so popular.

'David R. Ross is a proud patriot and unashamed romantic.'
SCOTLAND ON SUNDAY

'Robert the Bruce knew Scotland, knew every class of her people, as no man who ruled her before or since has done. It was he who asked of her a miracle - and she accomplished it.'
AGNES MUIR MACKENZIE

On the Trail of Mary Queen of Scots

J. Keith Cheetham
ISBN 0 946487 50 2 PBK £7.99

Life dealt Mary Queen of Scots love, intrigue, betrayal and tragedy in generous measure.

On the Trail of Mary Queen of Scots traces the major events in the turbulent life of the beautiful, enigmatic queen whose romantic reign and tragic destiny exerts an undimmed fascination over 400 years after her execution.

Places of interest to visit - 99 in Scotland, 35 in England and 29 in France.
One general map and 6 location maps.
Line drawings and illustrations.
Simplified family tree of the royal houses of Tudor and Stuart.
Key sites include:
Linlithgow Palace - Mary's birthplace, now a magnificent ruin
Stirling Castle - where, only nine months old, Mary was crowned Queen of Scotland
Notre Dame Cathedral - where, aged fifteen, she married the future king of France
The Palace of Holyroodhouse - Rizzio, one of Mary's closest advisers, was murdered here and some say his blood still stains the spot where he was stabbed to death
Sheffield Castle - where for fourteen years she languished as prisoner of her cousin, Queen Elizabeth I
Fotheringhay - here Mary finally met her death on the executioner's block.

On the Trail of Mary Queen of Scots is for everyone interested in the life of perhaps the most romantic figure in Scotland's history; a thorough guide to places connected with Mary, it is also a guide to the complexities of her personal and public life.

'In my end is my beginning'
MARY QUEEN OF SCOTS

'...the woman behaves like the Whore of Babylon' JOHN KNOX

On the Trail of Robert Service

GW Lockhart
ISBN 0 946487 24 3 PBK £7.99

Robert Service is famed world-wide for his eye-witness verse-pictures of the Klondike goldrush. As a war poet, his work outsold Owen and Sassoon, and he went on to become the world's first million selling poet. In search of adventure and new experiences, he emigrated from Scotland to Canada in 1890 where he was caught up in the aftermath of the raging gold fever. His vivid dramatic verse bring to life the wild, larger than life characters of the gold rush Yukon, their bar-room brawls, their lust for gold, their trigger-happy gambles with life and love. 'The Shooting of Dan McGrew' is perhaps his most famous poem:

A bunch of the boys were whooping it up in the Malamute saloon;
The kid that handles the music box was hitting a ragtime tune;
Back of the bar in a solo game, sat Dangerous Dan McGrew,
And watching his luck was his light o' love, the lady that's known as Lou.

His storytelling powers have brought Robert Service enduring fame, particularly in North America and Scotland where he is something of a cult figure.
Starting in Scotland, *On the Trail of Robert Service* follows Service as he wanders through British Columbia, Oregon, California, Mexico, Cuba, Tahiti, Russia, Turkey and the Balkans, finally 'settling' in France.
This revised edition includes an expanded selection of illustrations of scenes from the Klondike as well as several photographs from the family of Robert Service on his travels around the world.
Wallace Lockhart, an expert on Scottish traditional folk music and dance, is the author

of *Highland Balls & Village Halls* and *Fiddles & Folk*. His relish for a well-told tale in popular vernacular led him to fall in love with the verse of Robert Service and write his biography.

'*A fitting tribute to a remarkable man - a bank clerk who wanted to become a cowboy. It is hard to imagine a bank clerk writing such lines as:*

A bunch of boys were whooping it up...
The income from his writing actually exceeded his bank salary by a factor of five and he resigned to pursue a full time writing career.'
Charles Munn,
THE SCOTTISH BANKER

'*Robert Service claimed he wrote for those who wouldn't be seen dead reading poetry. His was an almost unbelievably mobile life... Lockhart hangs on breathlessly, enthusiastically unearthing clues to the poet's life.*' Ruth Thomas,
SCOTTISH BOOK COLLECTOR

'*This enthralling biography will delight Service lovers in both the Old World and the New.*'
Marilyn Wright,
SCOTS INDEPENDENT

On the Trail of John Muir

Cherry Good
ISBN 0 946487 62 6 PBK £7.99

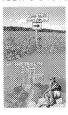

Follow the man who made the US go green. Confidant of presidents, father of American National Parks, trailblazer of world conservation and voted a Man of the Millennium in the US, John Muir's life and work is of continuing relevance. A man ahead of his time who saw the wilderness he loved threatened by industrialisation and determined to protect it, a crusade in which he was largely successful. His love of the wilderness began at an early age and he was filled with wanderlust all his life.

Only by going in silence, without baggage, can on truly get into the heart of the wilderness. All other travel is mere dust and hotels and baggage and chatter. JOHN MUIR

Braving mosquitoes and black bears Cherry Good set herself on his trail – Dunbar, Scotland; Fountain Lake and Hickory Hill, Wisconsin; Yosemite Valley and the Sierra Nevada, California; the Grand Canyon, Arizona; Alaska; and Canada – to tell his story. John Muir was himself a prolific

writer, and Good draws on his books, articles, letters and diaries to produce an account that is lively, intimate, humorous and anecdotal, and that provides refreshing new insights into the hero of world conservation.

John Muir chronology
General map plus 10 detailed maps covering the US, Canada and Scotland
Original colour photographs
Afterword advises on how to get involved
Conservation websites and addresses

Muir's importance has long been acknowledged in the US with over 200 sites of scenic beauty named after him. He was a Founder of The Sierra Club which now has over ¹/₂ million members. Due to the movement he started some 360 million acres of wilderness are now protected. This is a book which shows Muir not simply as a hero but as likeable humorous and self-effacing man of extraordinary vision.

'*I do hope that those who read this book will burn with the same enthusiasm for John Muir which the author shows.*'
WEST HIGHLAND FREE PRESS

On the Trail of Robert Burns

John Cairney
ISBN 0 946487 51 0 PBK £7.99

Is there anything new to say about Robert Burns?

John Cairney says it's time to trash Burns the Brand and come on the trail of the real Robert Burns. He is the best of travelling companions on this convivial, entertaining journey to the heart of the Burns story.

Internationally known as 'the face of Robert Burns', John Cairney believes that the traditional Burns tourist trail urgently needs to find a new direction. In an acting career spanning forty years he has often lived and breathed Robert Burns on stage. *On the Trail of Robert Burns* shows just how well he can get under the skin of a character. This fascinating journey around Scotland is a rediscovery of Scotland's national bard as a flesh and blood genius.

On the Trail of Robert Burns outlines five tours, mainly in Scotland. Key sites include:

Alloway - Burns' birthplace. 'Tam O'

Shanter' draws on the witch-stories about Alloway Kirk first heard by Burns in his childhood.

Mossgiel - between 1784 and 1786 in a phenomenal burst of creativity Burns wrote some of his most memorable poems including 'Holy Willie's Prayer' and 'To a Mouse.'

Kilmarnock - the famous Kilmarnock edition of *Poems Chiefly in the Scottish Dialect* published in 1786.

Edinburgh - fame and Clarinda (among others) embraced him.

Dumfries - Burns died at the age of 37. The trail ends at the Burns mausoleum in St Michael's churchyard.

'For me an aim I never fash
I rhyme for fun'.
ROBERT BURNS

'My love affair on stage with Burns started in London in 1959. It was consumated on stage at the Traverse Theatre in Edinburgh in 1965 and has continued happily ever since'.

JOHN CAIRNEY

'The trail is expertly, touchingly and amusingly followed'. THE HERALD

NATURAL SCOTLAND

Wild Scotland: The essential guide to finding the best of natural Scotland

James McCarthy
Photography by Laurie Campbell
ISBN 0 946487 37 5 PBK £7.50

With a foreword by Magnus Magnusson and striking colour photographs by Laurie Campbell, this is the essential up-to-date guide to viewing wildlife in Scotland for the visitor and resident alike. It provides a fascinating overview of the country's plants, animals, bird and marine life against the background of their typical natural settings, as an introduction to the vivid descriptions of the most accessible localities, linked to clear regional maps. A unique feature is the focus on 'green tourism' and sustainable visitor use of the countryside, contributed by Duncan Bryden, manager of the Scottish Tourist Board's Tourism and the Environment Task Force. Important practical information on access and the best times of year for viewing sites makes this an indispensable and user-friendly travelling companion to anyone interested in exploring Scotland's remarkable natural heritage.

James McCarthy is former Deputy Director for Scotland of the Nature Conservancy Council, and now a Board Member of Scottish Natural Heritage and Chairman of the Environmental Youth Work National Development Project Scotland.

'Nothing but Heather!'

Gerry Cambridge
ISBN 0 946487 49 9 PBK £15.00

Enter the world of Scottish nature – bizarre, brutal, often beautiful, always fascinating – as seen through the lens and poems of Gerry Cambridge, one of Scotland's most distinctive contemporary poets.

On film and in words, Cambridge brings unusual focus to bear on lives as diverse as those of dragonflies, hermit crabs, short-eared owls, and wood anemones. The result is both an instructive look by a naturalist at some of the flora and fauna of Scotland and a poet's aesthetic journey.

This exceptional collection comprises 48 poems matched with 48 captioned photographs. In his introduction Cambridge explores the origins of the project and the approaches to nature taken by other poets, and incorporates a wry account of an unwillingly-sectarian, farm-labouring, bird-obsessed adolescence in rural Ayrshire in the 1970s.

'Keats felt that the beauty of a rainbow was somehow tarnished by knowledge of its properties. Yet the natural world is surely made more, not less, marvellous by awareness of its workings. In the poems that accompany these pictures, I have tried to give an inkling of that. May the marriage of verse and image enlarge the reader's appreciation of and, perhaps, insight into the chomping, scurrying, quivering, procreating and dying kingdom, however many miles it be beyond the door.'
GERRY CAMBRIDGE

'a real poet, with a sense of the music of language and the poetry of life...' KATHLEEN RAINE

'one of the most promising and original of modern Scottish poets... a master of form and subtlety.'
GEORGE MACKAY BROWN

Scotland Land and People
An Inhabited Solitude

James McCarthy

ISBN 0 946487 57 X PBK £7.99

'Scotland is the country above all others that I have seen, in which a man of imagination may carve out his own pleasures; there are so many inhabited solitudes.'

DOROTHY WORDSWORTH, in her journal of August 1803

An informed and thought-provoking profile of Scotland's unique landscapes and the impact of humans on what we see now and in the future. James McCarthy leads us through the many aspects of the land and the people who inhabit it: natural Scotland; the rocks beneath; land ownership; the use of resources; people and place; conserving Scotland's heritage and much more.

Written in a highly readable style, this concise volume offers an under-standing of the land as a whole. Emphasising the uniqueness of the Scottish environment, the author explores the links between this and other aspects of our culture as a key element in rediscovering a modern sense of the Scottish identity and perception of nationhood.

'This book provides an engaging introduction to the mysteries of Scotland's people and landscapes. Difficult concepts are described in simple terms, providing the interested Scot or tourist with an invaluable overview of the country... It fills an important niche which, to my knowledge, is filled by no other publications.'

BETSY KING, Chief Executive, Scottish Environmental Education Council.

The Highland Geology Trail

John L Roberts

ISBN 0946487 36 7 PBK £4.99

Where can you find the oldest rocks in Europe? Where can you see ancient hills around 800 million years old? How do you tell whether a valley was carved out by a glacier, not a river? What are the Fucoid Beds?

Where do you find rocks folded like putty? How did great masses of rock pile up like snow in front of a snow-plough? When did volcanoes spew lava and ash to form Skye, Mull and Rum? Where can you find fossils on Skye?

'...a lucid introduction to the geological record in general, a jargon-free exposition of the regional background, and a series of descriptions of specific localities of geological interest on a 'trail' around the highlands.

Having checked out the local references on the ground, I can vouch for their accuracy and look forward to investigating farther afield, informed by this guide.

Great care has been taken to explain specific terms as they occur and, in so doing, John Roberts has created a resource of great value which is eminently usable by anyone with an interest in the outdoors...the best bargain you are likely to get as a geology book in the foreseeable future.'

Jim Johnston, PRESS AND JOURNAL

Rum: Nature's Island

Magnus Magnusson

ISBN 0 946487 32 4 £7.95 PBK

Rum: Nature's Island is the fascinating story of a Hebridean island from the earliest times through to the Clearances and its period as the sporting playground of a Lancashire industrial magnate, and on to its rebirth as a National Nature Reserve, a model for the active ecological management of Scotland's wild places.

Thoroughly researched and written in a lively accessible style, the book includes comprehensive coverage of the island's geology, animals and plants, and people, with a special chapter on the Edwardian extravaganza of Kinloch Castle. There is practical information for visitors to what was once known as 'the Forbidden Isle'; the book provides details of bothy and other accommodation, walks and nature trails. It closes with a positive vision for the island's future: biologically diverse, economically dynamic and ecologically sustainable.

Rum: Nature's Island is published in co-operation with Scottish Natural Heritage to mark the 40th anniversary of the acquisition of Rum by its predecessor, The Nature Conservancy.

Red Sky at Night

John Barrington

ISBN 0 946487 60 X   £8.99

'I read John Barrington's book with growing delight. This working shepherd writes beautifully about his animals, about the wildlife, trees and flowers which surround him at all times, and he paints an unforgettable picture of his glorious corner of Western Scotland. It is a lovely story of a rather wonderful life'.

JAMES HERRIOT

John Barrington is a shepherd to over 750 Blackface ewes who graze 2,000 acres of some of Britain's most beautiful hills overlooking the deep dark water of Loch Katrine in Perthshire. The yearly round of lambing, dipping, shearing and the sales is marvellously interwoven into the story of the glen, of Rob Roy in whose house John now lives, of curling when the ice is thick enough, and of sheep dog trials in the summer. Whether up to the hills or along the glen, John knows the haunts of the local wildlife: the wily hill fox, the grunting badger, the herds of red deer, and the shrews, voles and insects which scurry underfoot. He sets his seasonal clock by the passage of birds on the loch, and jealously guards over the golden eagle's eyrie in the hills. Paul Armstrong's sensitive illustrations are the perfect accompaniment to the evocative text.

'Mr Barrington is a great pleasure to read. One learns more things about the countryside from this account of one year than from a decade of The Archers'.

THE DAILY TELEGRAPH

'Powerful and evocative... a book which brings vividly to life the landscape, the wildlife, the farm animals and the people who inhabit John's vista. He makes it easy for the reader to fall in love with both his surrounds and his commune with nature'.

THE SCOTTISH FIELD

'An excellent and informative book.... not only an account of a shepherd's year but also the diary of a naturalist. Little escapes Barrington's enquiring eye and, besides the life cycle of a sheep, he gives those of every bird, beast, insect and plant that crosses his path, mixing their histories with descriptions of the geography, local history and folklore of his surroundings'.

TLS

'The family life at Glengyle is wholesome, appealing and not without a touch of the Good Life. Many will envy Mr Barrington his fastness home as they cruise up Loch Katrine on the tourist steamer'.

THE FIELD

Listen to the Trees

Don MacCaskill

ISBN 0 946487 65 0   £9.99 PBK

Don MacCaskill is one of Scotland's foremost naturalists, conservationists and wildlife photographers. *Listen to the Trees* is a beautiful and acutely observed account of how his outlook on life began to change as trees, woods, forests and all the wonders that they contain became a focus in his life. It is rich in its portrayal of the life that moves in the Caledonian forest and on the moorlands – lofty twig-stacked heronries, the elusive peregrine falcon and the red, bushy-tailed fox – of the beauty of the trees, and of those who worked in the forests.

'Trees are surely the supreme example of a life-force stronger than our own,' writes Don MacCaskill. 'Some, like the giant redwoods of North America, live for thousands of years. Some, like our own oaks and pines, may live for centuries. All, given the right conditions, will regenerate their species and survive long into the future.'

In the afterword Dr Philip Ratcliffe, former Head of the Forestry Commission's Environment Branch and a leading environment consultant, discusses the future role of Britain's forests – their influence on the natural environment and on the communities that live and work in and around them.

'Listen to the Trees will inspire all those with an interest in nature. It is a beautiful account, strongly anecdotal and filled with humour.'
RENNIE McOWAN

'This man adores trees. 200 years from now, your descendants will know why.'

JIM GILCHRIST, THE SCOTSMAN

LUATH GUIDES TO SCOTLAND

These guides are not your traditional where-to-stay and what-to-eat books. They are companions in the rucksack or car seat, providing the discerning traveller with a blend of fiery opinion and moving description. Here you will find '*that curious pastiche of myths and legend and history that the Scots use to describe their heritage... what battle happened in which glen between which clans; where the Picts sacrificed bulls as recently as the 17th century... A lively counterpoint to the more standard, detached guidebook... Intriguing.*'

THE WASHINGTON POST

These are perfect guides for the discerning visitor or resident to keep close by for reading again and again, written by authors who invite you to share their intimate knowledge and love of the areas covered.

Mull and Iona: Highways and Byways

Peter Macnab

ISBN 0 946487 58 8   PBK   £4.95

'The Isle of Mull is of Isles the fairest,
Of ocean's gems 'tis the first and rarest.'

So a local poet described it a hundred years ago, and this recently revised guide to Mull and sacred Iona, the most accessible islands of the Inner Hebrides, takes the reader on a delightful tour of these rare ocean gems, travelling with a native whose unparalleled knowledge and deep feeling for the area unlock the byways of the islands in all their natural beauty.

South West Scotland

Tom Atkinson

ISBN 0 946487 04 9   PBK   £4.95

This descriptive guide to the magical country of Robert Burns covers Kyle, Carrick, Galloway, Dumfriesshire, Kirkcudbrightshire and Wigtownshire. Hills, unknown moors and unspoiled beaches grace a land steeped in history and legend and portrayed with affection and deep delight.

An essential book for the visitor who yearns to feel at home in this land of peace and grandeur.

The West Highlands: The Lonely Lands

Tom Atkinson

ISBN 0 946487 56 1   PBK   £4.95

A guide to Inveraray, Glencoe, Loch Awe, Loch Lomond, Cowal, the Kyles of Bute and all of central Argyll written with insight, sympathy and loving detail. Once Atkinson has taken you there, these lands can never feel lonely. 'I have sought to make the complex simple, the beautiful accessible and the strange familiar,' he writes, and indeed he brings to the land a knowledge and affection only accessible to someone with intimate knowledge of the area.

A must for travellers and natives who want to delve beneath the surface.

'*Highly personal and somewhat quirky... steeped in the lore of Scotland.*'
THE WASHINGTON POST

The Northern Highlands: The Empty Lands

Tom Atkinson

ISBN 0 946487 55 3   PBK   £4.95

The Highlands of Scotland from Ullapool to Bettyhill and Bonar Bridge to John O' Groats are landscapes of myth and legend, 'empty of people, but of nothing else that brings delight to any tired soul,' writes Atkinson. This highly personal guide describes Highland history and landscape with love, compassion and above all sheer magic.

Essential reading for anyone who has dreamed of the Highlands.

The North West Highlands: Roads to the Isles

Tom Atkinson

ISBN 0 946487 54 5   PBK   £4.95

Ardnamurchan, Morvern, Morar, Moidart and the west coast to Ullapool are included in this guide to the Far West and Far North of Scotland. An unspoiled land of mountains, lochs and silver sands is brought to the walker's toe-tips (and to the reader's fingertips) in this stark, serene and evocative account of town, country and legend.

For any visitor to this Highland wonderland, Queen Victoria's favourite place on earth.

WALK WITH LUATH

Mountain Days & Bothy Nights

Dave Brown and Ian Mitchell

ISBN 0 946487 15 4 PBK £7.50

Acknowledged as a classic of mountain writing still in demand ten years after its first publication, this book takes you into the bothies, howffs and dosses on the Scottish hills. Fishgut Mac, Desperate Dan and Stumpy the Big Yin stalk hill and public house, evading gamekeepers and Royalty with a camaraderie which was the trademark of Scots hillwalking in the early days.

'*The fun element comes through... how innocent the social polemic seems in our nastier world of today... the book for the rucksack this year.*'
Hamish Brown,
SCOTTISH MOUNTAINEERING
CLUB JOURNAL

The Joy of Hillwalking

Ralph Storer

ISBN 0 946487 28 6 PBK £7.50

Apart, perhaps, from the joy of sex, the joy of hillwalking brings more pleasure to more people than any other form of human activity.

'*Alps, America, Scandinavia, you name it – Storer's been there, so why the hell shouldn't he bring all these various and varied places into his observations... [He] even admits to losing his virginity after a day on the Aggy Ridge... Well worth its place alongside Storer's earlier works.*' TAC

Scotland's Mountains before the Mountaineers

Ian Mitchell

ISBN 0 946487 39 1 PBK £9.99

In this ground-breaking book, Ian Mitchell tells the story of explorations and ascents in the Scottish Highlands in the days before

mountaineering became a popular sport – when bandits, Jacobites, poachers and illicit distillers traditionally used the mountains as sanctuary. The book also gives a detailed account of the map makers, road builders, geologists, astronomers and naturalists, many of whom ascended hitherto untrodden summits while working in the Scottish Highlands.

Scotland's Mountains before the Mountaineers is divided into four Highland regions, with a map of each region showing key summits. While not designed primarily as a guide, it will be a useful handbook for walkers and climbers. Based on a wealth of new research, this book offers a fresh perspective that will fascinate climbers and mountaineers and everyone interested in the history of mountaineering, cartography, the evolution of landscape and the social history of the Scottish Highlands.

LUATH WALKING GUIDES

The highly respected and continually updated guides to the Cairngorms.

'*Particularly good on local wildlife and how to see it*' THE COUNTRYMAN

Walks in the Cairngorms

Ernest Cross

ISBN 0 946487 09 X PBK £4.95

This selection of walks celebrates the rare birds, animals, plants and geological wonders of a region often believed difficult to penetrate on foot. Nothing is difficult with this guide in your pocket, as Cross gives a choice for every walker, and includes valuable tips on mountain safety and weather advice.

Ideal for walkers of all ages and skiers waiting for snowier skies.

Short Walks in the Cairngorms

Ernest Cross

ISBN 0 946487 23 5 PBK £4.95

Cross wrote this volume after overhearing a walker remark that there were no short walks for lazy ramblers in the Cairngorm region.

Here is the answer: rambles through scenic woods with a welcoming pub at the end, birdwatching hints, glacier holes, or for the fit and ambitious, scrambles up hills to admire vistas of glorious scenery. Wildlife in the Cairngorms is unequalled elsewhere in Britain, and here it is brought to the binoculars of any walker who treads quietly and with respect.

FOLKLORE

The Supernatural Highlands

Francis Thompson

ISBN 0 946487 31 6 PBK £8.99

An authoritative exploration of the otherworld of the Highlander, happenings and beings hitherto thought to be outwith the ordinary forces of nature. A simple introduction to the way of life of rural Highland and Island communities, this new edition weaves a path through second sight, the evil eye, witchcraft, ghosts, fairies and other supernatural beings, offering new sight-lines on areas of belief once dismissed as folklore and superstition.

Scotland: Myth, Legend and Folklore

Stuart McHardy

ISBN: 0 946487 69 3 PBK 7.99

Who were the people who built the megaliths? What great warriors sleep beneath the Hollow Hills? Were the early Scottish saints just pagans in disguise?

Was King Arthur really Scottish? When was Nessie first sighted?

This is a book about Scotland drawn from hundreds, if not thousands of years of storytelling. From the oral traditions of the Scots, Gaelic and Norse speakers of the past, it presents a new picture of who the Scottish are and where they come from. The stories that McHardy recounts may be hilarious, tragic, heroic, frightening or just plain bizzare, but

they all provide an insight into a unique tradition of myth, legend and folklore that has marked both the language and landscape of Scotland.

Tall Tales from an Island

Peter Macnab

ISBN 0 946487 07 3 PBK £8.99

Peter Macnab was born and reared on Mull. He heard many of these tales as a lad, and others he has listened to in later years.

There are humorous tales, grim tales, witty tales, tales of witchcraft, tales of love, tales of heroism, tales of treachery, historical tales and tales of yesteryear.

A popular lecturer, broadcaster and writer, Peter Macnab is the author of a number of books and articles about Mull, the island he knows so intimately and loves so much. As he himself puts it in his introduction to this book 'I am of the unswerving opinion that nowhere else in the world will you find a better way of life, nor a finer people with whom to share it.'

'All islands, it seems, have a rich store of characters whose stories represent a kind of sub-culture without which island life would be that much poorer. Macnab has succeeded in giving the retelling of the stories a special Mull flavour, so much so that one can visualise the storytellers sitting on a bench outside the house with a few cronies, puffing on their pipes and listening with nodding approval.'

WEST HIGHLAND FREE PRESS

Tales from the North Coast

Alan Temperley

ISBN 0 946487 18 9 PBK £8.99

Seals and shipwrecks, witches and fairies, curses and clearances, fact and fantasy – the authentic tales in this collection come straight from the heart of a small Highland community. Children and adults alike responsd to their timeless appeal. These *Tales of the North Coast* were collected in the early 1970s by Alan Temperley and young people at Farr Secondary School in Sutherland. All the stories were gathered from the area between the

Kyle of Tongue and Strath Halladale, in scattered communities wonderfully rich in lore that had been passed on by word of mouth down the generations. This wide-ranging selection provides a satisying balance between intriguing tales of the supernatural and more everyday occurrences. The book also includes chilling eye-witness accounts of the notorious Strathnaver Clearances when tenants were given a few hours to pack up and get out of their homes, which were then burned to the ground.

Underlying the continuity through the generations, this new edition has a foreward by Jim Johnston, the head teacher at Farr, and includes the vigorous linocut images produced by the young people under the guidance of their art teacher, Elliot Rudie.

Since the original publication of this book, Alan Temperley has gone on to become a highly regarded writer for children.

'The general reader will find this book's spontaneity, its pictures by the children and its fun utterly charming.' SCOTTISH REVIEW

'An admirable book which should serve as an encouragement to other districts to gather what remains of their heritage of folk-tales.'
SCOTTISH EDUCATION JOURNAL

NEW SCOTLAND

Scotland - Land and Power
the agenda for land reform

Andy Wightman
in association with
Democratic Left Scotland
foreword by Lesley Riddoch
ISBN 0 946487 70 7 PBK £5.00

What is land reform? Why is it needed? Will the Scottish Parliament really make a difference?

Scotland – Land and Power argues passionately that nothing less than a radical, comprehensive programme of land reform can make the difference that is needed. Now is no time for palliative solutions which treat the symptoms and not the causes.

Scotland – Land and Power is a controversial and provocative book that clarifies the complexities of landownership in Scotland. Andy Wightman explodes the myth that land issues are relevant only to the far flung fringes of rural Scotland, and questions mainstream political commitment to land

reform. He presents his own far-reaching programme for change and a pragmatic, inspiring vision of how Scotland can move from outmoded, unjust power structures towards a more equitable landowning democracy.

'Writers like Andy Wightman are determined to make sure that the hurt of the last century is not compounded by a rushed solution in the next. This accessible, comprehensive but passionately argued book is quite simply essential reading and perfectly timed – here's hoping Scotland's legislators agree.'
LESLEY RIDDOCH

Old Scotland New Scotland

Jeff Fallow
ISBN 0 946487 40 5 PBK £6.99

'Together we can build a new Scotland based on Labour's values.' DONALD DEWAR, Party Political Broad-cast

'Despite the efforts of decent Mr Dewar, the voters may yet conclude they are looking at the same old hacks in brand new suits.' IAN BELL, *The Independent*

'At times like this you suddenly realise how dangerous the neglect of Scottish history in our schools and universities may turn out to be.'

MICHAEL FRY, *The Herald*

'...one of the things I hope will go is our chip on the shoulder about the English... The SNP has a huge responsibility to articulate Scottish independence in a way that is pro-Scottish and not anti-English.'

ALEX SALMOND, *The Scotsman*

Scottish politics have never been more exciting. In *old Scotland new Scotland* Jeff Fallow takes us on a graphic voyage through Scotland's turbulent history, from earliest times through to the present day and beyond. This fast-track guide is the quick way to learn what your history teacher didn't tell you, essential reading for all who seek an understanding of Scotland and its history.

Eschewing the romanticisation of his country's past, Fallow offers a new perspective on an old nation. *'Too many people associate Scottish history with tartan trivia or outworn romantic myth. This book aims to blast that stubborn idea.'* JEFF FALLOW

Notes from the North
incorporating a Brief History of the Scots and the English
Emma Wood

ISBN 0 946487 46 4 PBK £8.99

Notes on being English
Notes on being in Scotland
Learning from a shared past

Sickened by the English jingoism that surfaced in rampant form during the 1982 Falklands War, Emma Wood started to dream of moving from her home in East Anglia to the Highlands of Scotland. She felt increasingly frustrated and marginalised as Thatcherism got a grip on the southern English psyche. The Scots she met on frequent holidays in the Highlands had no truck with Thatcherism, and she felt at home with grass-roots Scottish anti-authoritarianism. The decision was made. She uprooted and headed for a new life in the north of Scotland.

'An intelligent and perceptive book... calm, reflective, witty and sensitive. It should certainly be read by all English visitors to Scotland, be they tourists or incomers. And it should certainly be read by all Scots concerned about what kind of nation we live in. They might learn something about themselves.'
THE HERALD

'... her enlightenment is evident on every page of this perceptive, provocative book.'
MAIL ON SUNDAY

FICTION
The Bannockburn Years
William Scott
ISBN 0 946487 34 0 PRK £7.95

A present day Edinburgh solicitor stumbles across reference to a document of value to the Nation State of Scotland. He tracks down the document on the Isle of Bute, a document which probes the real 'quaestiones' about nationhood and national identity. The document ends up being published, but is it authentic and does it matter? Almost 700 years on, these 'quaestiones' are still worth asking.

Written with pace and passion, William

Scott has devised an intriguing vehicle to open up new ways of looking at the future of Scotland and its people. He presents an alternative interpretation of how the Battle of Bannockburn was fought, and through the Bannatyne manuscript he draws the reader into the minds of those involved.

Winner of the 1997 Constable Trophy, the premier award in Scotland for an unpublished novel, this book offers new insights to both the academic and the general reader which are sure to provoke further discussion and debate.

'A brilliant storyteller. I shall expect to see your name writ large hereafter.'
NIGEL TRANTER, October 1997.

'... a compulsive read.' PH Scott, THE SCOTSMAN

The Great Melnikov
Hugh Maclachlan
ISBN 0 946487 42 1 PBK £7.95

A well crafted, gripping novel, written in a style reminiscent of John Buchan and set in London and the Scottish Highlands during the First World War, *The Great Melnikov* is a dark tale of double-cross and deception. We first meet Melnikov, one-time star of the German circus, languishing as a down-and-out in Trafalgar Square. He soon finds himself drawn into a tortuous web of intrigue. He is a complex man whose personal struggle with alcoholism is an inner drama which parallels the tense twists and turns as a spy mystery unfolds. Melnikov's options are narrowing. The circle of threat is closing. Will Melnikov outwit the sinister enemy spy network? Can he summon the will and the wit to survive?

Hugh Maclachlan, in his first full length novel, demonstrates an undoubted ability to tell a good story well. His earlier stories have been broadcast on Radio Scotland, and he has the rare distinction of being shortlisted for the Macallan/Scotland on Sunday Short Story Competition two years in succession.

'... a satisfying rip-roarer of a thriller... an undeniable page turner, racing along to a suitably cinematic ending, richly descriptive yet clear and lean.'
THE SCOTSMAN

Grave Robbers

Robin Mitchell

ISBN 0 946487 72 3 PBK £7.95

After years of sleeping peacefully, the deceased dignitaries of Old Edinburgh are about to get a nasty surprise...
Grave-digger and funeral enthusiast Cameron Carter lives a relatively quiet life.
Until a misplaced shovel cracks open a coffin lid and reveals a hidden fortune, that is. Nearly one hundred and seventy years after the trial of Scotland's notorious body snatchers, William Burke and William Hare, the ancient trade of grave robbing returns to the town's cemeteries.

Forming an unholy union with small time crook, Adam, Cameron is drawn into a web of crime that involves a bogus American Scholars' Society, chocolate chip ice cream and Steve McQueen. Their sacrilegious scheming doesn't go quite to plan, however, and events begin to spiral dangerously beyond Cameron the answers will be exhumed.

Will our hero pull the tour guide of his dreams?

Will his partner in crime ever shift those microwaves?

Is there an afterlife?

In Robin Mitchell's rude and darkly comic debut novel, all the answers will be exhumed.

'*Good, unclean macabre fun from Robin Mitchell...*'
IAN RANKIN

But n Ben A-Go-Go

Matthew Fitt

ISBN 0 946487 82 0 HBK £10.99

The year is 2090. Global flooding has left most of Scotland under water. The descendants of those who survived God's Flood live in a community of floating island parishes, known collectively as Port.

Port's citizens live in mortal fear of Senga, a supervirus whose victims are kept in a giant hospital warehouse in sealed capsules called Kists.

Paolo Broon is a low-ranking cyberjanny. His life-partner, Nadia, lies forgotten and alone in Omega Kist 624 in the Rigo Imbeki Medical Center. When he receives an unexpected message from his radge criminal father to meet him at But n Ben A-Go-Go, Paolo's life is changed forever.

He must traverse VINE, Port and the Drylands and deal with rebel American tourists and crabbit Dundonian microchips to discover the truth about his family's past in order to free Nadia from the sair grip of the merciless Senga.

Set in a distinctly unbonnie future-Scotland, the novel's dangerous atmosphere and psychologically-malkied characters weave a tale that both chills and intrigues. In *But n Ben A-Go-Go* Matthew Fitt takes the allegedly dead language of Scots and energises it with a narrative that crackles and fizzes with life.

'*After an initial shock, readers of this sprightly and imaginative tale will begin to relish its verbal impetus, where a standard Lallans, laced with bits of Dundonian and Aberdonian, is stretched and skelped to meet the demands of cyberjannies and virtual hoorhooses.*

Eurobawbees, rooburgers, mutant kelpies, and titanic blooters from supertyphoons make sure that the Scottish peninsula is no more parochial than its language. I recommend an entertaining and ground-breaking book.'
EDWIN MORGAN

'*Matthew Fitt's instinctive use of Scots is spellbinding. This is an assured novel of real inventiveness. Be prepared to boldly go...*'
ELLIE McDONALD

'*Easier to read than Shakespeare – wice the fun.*'
DES DILLON

HISTORY

Blind Harry's Wallace

William Hamilton of Gilbertfield

Introduced by Elspeth King

ISBN 0 946487 43 X HBK £15.00
ISBN 0 946487 33 2 PBK £8.99

The original story of the real braveheart, Sir William Wallace. Racy, blood on every page, violently anglophobic, grossly embellished, vulgar and disgusting, clumsy and stilted, a literary failure, a great epic.

Whatever the verdict on BLIND HARRY, this is the book which has done more than any other to frame the notion of Scotland's national identity. Despite its numerous 'historical inaccuracies', it remains the principal source for what we now know about the life of Wallace.

The novel and film *Braveheart* were based on the 1722 Hamilton edition of this epic poem.

Burns, Wordsworth, Byron and others were greatly influenced by this version 'wherein the old obsolete words are rendered more intelligible', which is said to be the book, next to the Bible, most commonly found in Scottish households in the eighteenth century. Burns even admits to having 'borrowed... a couplet worthy of Homer' directly from Hamilton's version of BLIND HARRY to include in '*Scots wha hae*'.

Elspeth King, in her introduction to this, the first accessible edition of BLIND HARRY in verse form since 1859, draws parallels between the situation in Scotland at the time of Wallace and that in Bosnia and Chechnya in the 1990s. Seven hundred years to the day after the Battle of Stirling Bridge, the 'Settled Will of the Scottish People' was expressed in the devolution referendum of 11 September 1997. She describes this as a landmark opportunity for mature reflection on how the nation has been shaped, and sees BLIND HARRY'S WALLACE as an essential and compelling text for this purpose.

'*A true bard of the people*'.
TOM SCOTT, THE PENGUIN BOOK OF SCOTTISH VERSE, on Blind Harry.

'*A more inventive writer than Shakespeare*'.
RANDALL WALLACE

'*The story of Wallace poured a Scottish prejudice in my veins which will boil along until the floodgates of life shut in eternal rest*'.
ROBERT BURNS

'*Hamilton's couplets are not the best poetry you will ever read, but they rattle along at a fair pace. In re-issuing this work, the publishers have re-opened the spring from which most of our conceptions of the Wallace legend come*'.
SCOTLAND ON SUNDAY

'*The return of Blind Harry's Wallace, a man who makes Mel look like a wimp*'.
THE SCOTSMAN

Reportage Scotland: History in the Making

Louise Yeoman
Foreword by Professor David Stevenson
ISBN 0 946487 61 8 PBK £9.99

Events – both major and minor – as seen and recorded by Scots throughout history.

Which king was murdered in a sewer?
What was Dr Fian's love magic?
Who was the half-roasted abbot?

Which cardinal was salted and put in a barrel?
Why did Lord Kitchener's niece try to blow up Burns's cottage?

The answers can all be found in this eclectic mix covering nearly 2000 years of Scottish history. Historian Louise Yeoman's rummage through the manuscript, book and newspaper archives of the National Library of Scotland has yielded an astonishing range of material from a letter to the king of the Picts to in Mary Queen of Scots' own account of the murder of David Riccio; from the execution of William Wallace to accounts of anti-poll tax actions and the opening of the new Scottish Parliament. The book takes pieces from the original French, Latin, Gaelic and Scots and makes them accessible to the general reader, often for the first time.

The result is compelling reading for anyone interested in the history that has made Scotland what it is today.

'*Marvellously illuminating and wonderfully readable*'. Angus Calder, SCOTLAND ON SUNDAY

'*A monumental achievement in drawing together such a rich historical harvest*'
Chris Holme,
THE HERALD

SOCIAL HISTORY

A Word for Scotland

Jack Campbell
with a foreword by Magnus Magnusson
ISBN 0 946487 48 0 PBK £12.99

'A word for Scotland' was Lord Beaver-brook's hope when he founded the *Scottish Daily Express*. That word for Scotland quickly became, and was for many years, the national newspaper of Scotland.

The pages of *A Word For Scotland* exude warmth and a wry sense of humour. Jack Campbell takes us behind the scenes to meet the larger-than-life characters and ordinary people who made and recorded the stories. Here we hear the stories behind the stories that hit the headlines in this great yarn of journalism in action.

It would be true to say 'all life is here'. From the Cheapside Street fire of which cost the lives of 19 Glasgow firemen, to the theft of the Stone of Destiny, to the lurid exploits of serial killer Peter Manuel, to encounters with world boxing champions Benny Lynch and Cassius Clay - this book offers telling glimpses of the characters, events, joy and tragedy which make up Scotland's story in the 20th century.

'As a rookie reporter you were proud to work on it and proud to be part of it - it was fine newspaper right at the heartbeat of Scotland.'

RONALD NEIL, Chief Executive of BBC Production, and a reporter on the *Scottish Daily Express* (1963-68)

'This book is a fascinating reminder of Scottish journalism in its heyday. It will be read avidly by those journalists who take pride in their profession – and should be compulsory reading for those who don't.'

JACK WEBSTER, columnist on *The Herald* and *Scottish Daily Express* journalist (1960-80)

The Crofting Years

Francis Thompson

ISBN 0 946487 06 5 PBK £6.95

Crofting is much more than a way of life. It is a storehouse of cultural, linguistic and moral values which holds together a scattered and struggling rural population. This book fills a blank in the written history of crofting over the last two centuries. Bloody conflicts and gunboat diplomacy, treachery, compassion, music and story: all figure in this mine of information on crofting in the Highlands and Islands of Scotland.

'I would recommend this book to all who are interested in the past, but even more so to those who are interested in the future survival of our way of life and culture'
STORNOWAY GAZETTE

'The book is a mine of information on many aspects of the past, among them the homes, the food, the music and the medicine of our crofting forebears.'
John M Macmillan, erstwhile CROFTERS COMMISSIONER FOR LEWIS AND HARRIS

Shale Voices

Alistair Findlay
foreword by Tam Dalyell MP
ISBN 0 946487 63 4 PBK £10.99
ISBN 0 946487 78 2 HBK £17.99

'He was at Addiewell oil works. Anyone goes in there is there for keeps.'
JOE, Electrician

'There's shale from here to Ayr, you see.'
DICK, a Drawer

'The way I describe it is, you're a coal miner and I'm a shale miner. You're a tramp and I'm a toff.'
HARRY, a Drawer

'There were sixteen or eighteen Simpsons...
...She was having one every dividend we would say.'
SISTERS, from Broxburn

Shale Voices offers a fascinating insight into shale mining, an industry that employed generations of Scots, had an impact on the social, political and cultural history of Scotland and gave birth to today's large oil companies. Author Alistair Findlay was born in the shale mining village of Winchburgh and is the fourth son of a shale miner, Bob Findlay, who became editor of the *West Lothian Courier*. *Shale Voices* combines oral history, local journalism and family history. The generations of communities involved in shale mining provide, in their own words, a unique documentation of the industry and its cultural and political impact.

Photographs, drawings, poetry and short stories make this a thought provoking and entertaining account. It is as much a joy to dip into and feast the eyes on as to read from cover to cover.

'Alistair Findlay has added a basic source material to the study of Scottish history that is invaluable and will be of great benefit to future generations. Scotland owes him a debt of gratitude for undertaking this work.' TAM DALYELL MP

TRAVEL & LEISURE
Edinburgh and Leith Pub Guide

Stuart McHardy
ISBN 0 946487 80 4 PBK £4.95

You might be in Edinburgh to explore the closes and wynds of one of Europe's most beautiful cities, to sample the finest Scotch whiskies and to discover a rich Celtic heritage of traditional music and storytelling. Or you might be in Leith to get trashed. Either way, this is the guide for you.

With the able assistance of his long time drinking partner, 'the Man from Fife', Stuart McHardy has dragged his tired old frame around over two hundred pubs – all in the name of research, of course. Alongside drinking numerous pints, he has managed to compile enough historical anecdote and practical information to allow anyone with a sturdy liver to follow in his footsteps.

Although Stuart unashamedly gives top marks to his favourite haunts, he rates most highly those pubs that are original, distinctive and cater to the needs of their clientele. Be it domino league or play-station league, pina colada or a pint of heavy, filled foccacia or mince and tatties, Stuart has found a decent pub that does it.

Over 200 pubs
12 pub trails plus maps
Helpful rating system
Brief guide to Scottish beers and whiskies
'The Man from Fife's wry take on each pub
Discover the answers to such essential questions as:
Which pubs are recommended by whisky wholesalers for sampling?
Where can you find a pub that has links with Bonnie Prince Charlie and Mary Queen of Scots?
Which pub serves kangaroo burgers?
Where can you go for a drop of mead in Edinburgh?
Which pub has a toy crocodile in pride of place behind the bar?
How has Stuart survived all these years?
Long familiar with Edinburgh and Leith's drinking dens, watering holes, shebeens and dens of iniquity, Stuart McHardy has penned a bible for the booze connoisseur. Whether you're here for Hogmanay, a Six Nations weekend, the Festival, just one evening or the rest of your life, this is the companion to slip in your pocket or handbag as you venture out in search of the craic.

Edinburgh's Historic Mile
Duncan Priddle
ISBN 0 946487 97 9 PBK £2.99

 This ancient thoroughfare runs downwards and eastwards for just over a mile. Its narrow closes and wynds, each with a distinctive atmosphere and character, have their own stories to tell. From the looming fortress of the Castle at the top, to the Renaissance beauty of the palace at the bottom, every step along this ancient highway brings the city's past to life – a past both glorious and gory.
Written with all the knowledge and experience that the Witchery Tours have gathered in 15 years, it is full of quirky, fun and fascinating stories that you wont find anywhere else.
Designed to fit easily in pocket or bag and with a comprehensive map on the back cover this is the perfect book to take on a walk in Edinburgh or read before you arrive.

Pilgrims In The Rough:
St Andrews beyond the 19th hole
Michael Tobert
ISBN 0 946487 74 X PBK £7.99
'A travel book about St. Andrews. A book that

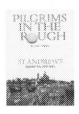 combines the game I love and the course I have played for 20 years, with the town that I consider as close to paradise as I am likely to find on this side of the pearly gates.'
MICHAEL TOBERT

With ghosts, witches and squabbling clerics, Pilgrims in the Rough is a funny and affectionate portrayal of Michael Tobert's home town. The author has always wanted to write a travel book – but he has done more than that. Combining tourist information with history, humour and anecdote, he has written a book that will appeal to golfer and non golfer, local and visitor, alike.

While Pilgrims in the Rough is more than just a guide to clubs and caddies, it is nonetheless packed with information for the golf enthusiast. It features a detailed map of the course and the low down from a regular St Andrews player on booking times, the clubs and each of the holes on the notorious Old Course.

The book also contains an informative guide to the attractions of the town and the best places to stay and to eat out. Michael Tobert's infectious enthusiasm for St Andrews will even persuade the most jaded golf widow or widower that the town is worth a visit!

'An extraordinary book' THE OBSERVER

'Tobert displays genuine erudition on such topics as the history of the cathedral and university and, of course, the tricky business of playing the Old Course itself.' THE SCOTSMAN

POETRY
Poems to be read aloud

Collected and with an introduction by Tom Atkinson
ISBN 0 946487 00 6 PBK £5.00

 This personal collection of doggerel and verse ranging from the tear-jerking Green Eye of the Yellow God to the rarely printed, bawdy Eskimo Nell has a lively cult following. Much borrowed and rarely returned, this is a book for reading aloud in very good company, preferably after a dram or twa. You are guaranteed a warm welcome if you arrive at a gathering with this little volume in your pocket.

Luath Press Limited
committed to publishing well written books worth reading

LUATH PRESS takes its name from Robert Burns, whose little collie Luath (*Gael.*, swift or nimble) tripped up Jean Armour at a wedding and gave him the chance to speak to the woman who was to be his wife and the abiding love of his life. Burns called one of *The Twa Dogs* Luath after Cuchullin's hunting dog in *Ossian's Fingal*. Luath Press grew up in the heart of Burns country, and now resides a few steps up the road from Burns' first lodgings in Edinburgh's Royal Mile.

Luath offers you distinctive writing with a hint of unexpected pleasures.

Most UK and US bookshops either carry our books in stock or can order them for you. To order direct from us, please send a £sterling cheque, postal order, international money order or your credit card details (number, address of cardholder and expiry date) to us at the address below. Please add post and packing as follows: UK – £1.00 per delivery address; overseas surface mail – £2.50 per delivery address; overseas airmail – £3.50 for the first book to each delivery address, plus £1.00 for each additional book by airmail to the same address. If your order is a gift, we will happily enclose your card or message at no extra charge.

Luath Press Limited
543/2 Castlehill
The Royal Mile
Edinburgh EH1 2ND
Scotland
Telephone: 0131 225 4326 (24 hours)
Fax: 0131 225 4324
email: gavin.macdougall@luath.co.uk
Website: www.luath.co.uk